MW01539048

Brazil

Everything You Need to Know

Copyright © 2024 by Noah Gil-Smith.

All rights reserved. No part of this book may be reproduced, distributed, or transmitted in any form or by any means, including photocopying, recording, or other electronic or mechanical methods, without the prior written permission of the publisher, except in the case of brief quotations embodied in critical reviews and certain other noncommercial uses permitted by copyright law. This book was created with the assistance of Artificial Intelligence. The content presented in this book is for entertainment purposes only. It should not be considered as a substitute for professional advice or comprehensive research. Readers are encouraged to independently verify any information and consult relevant experts for specific matters. The author and publisher disclaim any liability or responsibility for any loss, injury, or inconvenience caused or alleged to be caused directly or indirectly by the information presented in this book.

4

Introduction to Brazil

Brazil, the largest country in South America, captivates with its immense size, diverse landscapes, and vibrant culture. Nestled in the heart of the continent, Brazil spans nearly half of South America's landmass, boasting a territory rich in natural wonders, from the lush Amazon rainforest to the golden sands of its coastline.

With a population of over 200 million people, Brazil is a melting pot of cultures and ethnicities, shaped by centuries of indigenous heritage, European colonization, African slavery, and waves of immigration from around the world. This multicultural tapestry weaves its way through every aspect of Brazilian life, from its music and cuisine to its language and traditions.

The history of Brazil is a tale of exploration, conquest, and resilience. Indigenous peoples inhabited the land for thousands of years before Portuguese explorers arrived in the early 16th century, drawn by the promise of riches and adventure. The Portuguese colonization left an indelible mark on Brazil, shaping its language, religion, and society.

In 1822, Brazil declared its independence from Portugal, establishing itself as a monarchy before transitioning to a republic in 1889. Throughout the 20th century, Brazil underwent significant political and social upheaval, from military dictatorships to periods of democratic reform. Today, Brazil stands as a vibrant democracy, navigating the complexities of modern governance while striving to address longstanding issues of inequality and social justice.

From the dense jungles of the Amazon to the bustling metropolises of Rio de Janeiro and São Paulo, Brazil's geography is as diverse as its people. The Amazon rainforest, often referred to as the "lungs of the planet," is home to an astonishing array of flora and fauna, including countless species found nowhere else on Earth. Brazil's coastline stretches for over 7,000 kilometers, offering pristine beaches, coral reefs, and vibrant coastal cities.

Brazilian culture is renowned for its passion, creativity, and diversity. Music pulses through the streets of Brazil, from the rhythms of samba and bossa nova to the beats of funk and forró. Cuisine is a celebration of flavors and traditions, blending indigenous, African, European, and Asian influences into a rich tapestry of dishes and delicacies.

Language is a cornerstone of Brazilian identity, with Portuguese serving as the official tongue. Brazilian Portuguese has its own unique accents, expressions, and idioms, reflecting the country's distinct regional cultures and dialects.

As we embark on this journey through Brazil, we'll delve into its history, geography, culture, and people, exploring the vibrant tapestry of experiences that make this country unlike any other. Join us as we uncover the sights, sounds, and stories of Brazil, a land of endless wonder and boundless possibility.

Geographical Overview: From the Amazon to the Atlantic

Brazil's geographical landscape is a mosaic of diverse ecosystems and breathtaking vistas, stretching from the dense rainforests of the Amazon to the sun-drenched shores of the Atlantic Ocean. At the heart of Brazil lies the Amazon Basin, home to the world's largest tropical rainforest. Spanning over 6.7 million square kilometers, the Amazon rainforest teems with an astonishing array of plant and animal life, from towering canopy trees to elusive jaguars and vibrant macaws.

To the south of the Amazon Basin lies the Brazilian Highlands, a vast plateau characterized by rolling hills, rugged mountains, and fertile valleys. The Highlands are the source of Brazil's major rivers, including the Amazon, Paraná, and São Francisco, which carve their way through the landscape, shaping the country's geography and providing vital resources for agriculture, industry, and transportation.

Along Brazil's eastern coast stretches the Atlantic Coastal Plain, a narrow strip of land bordered by the Atlantic Ocean to the east and the Brazilian Highlands to the west. This coastal region is home to Brazil's largest cities, including Rio de Janeiro, São Paulo, and Salvador, as well as some of the country's most iconic landmarks and tourist attractions.

The Amazon River, the lifeline of the rainforest, winds its way through Brazil's northern region, flowing over 6,575 kilometers from its source in the Peruvian Andes to its mouth in the Atlantic Ocean. Along its journey, the Amazon River branches into a vast network of tributaries, creating a complex ecosystem of rivers, lakes, and wetlands that support an extraordinary diversity of aquatic life.

In the northeast of Brazil lies the semi-arid region known as the Sertão, characterized by its harsh climate, sparse vegetation, and rugged terrain. Despite its arid conditions, the Sertão is home to resilient communities and unique ecosystems, including the Caatinga biome, a thorny scrubland that is found nowhere else on Earth.

To the south of the Brazilian Highlands lies the Pantanal, the world's largest tropical wetland area. Covering an area of over 150,000 square kilometers, the Pantanal is a biodiversity hotspot, home to an incredible array of wildlife, including jaguars, caimans, and giant otters.

Brazil's geographical diversity is further enhanced by its coastal islands, including Fernando de Noronha, Ilha Grande, and Marajó, each offering its own unique blend of natural beauty and cultural heritage.

From the towering peaks of the Andes to the sun-kissed beaches of the Atlantic coast, Brazil's geography is as varied and vibrant as its people and culture. Join us as we explore the breathtaking landscapes and natural wonders that make Brazil one of the most enchanting destinations on Earth.

Historical Foundations: Indigenous Peoples and Early Settlements

To understand Brazil's historical foundations, we must delve into the rich tapestry of its indigenous peoples and early settlements. Long before the arrival of European explorers, the land we now know as Brazil was inhabited by diverse indigenous cultures, each with its own languages, customs, and traditions. These indigenous peoples, including the Tupinambá, Guarani, and Tupiniquim, thrived in harmony with the land, building complex societies based on agriculture, hunting, and fishing.

The first Europeans to reach Brazil were Portuguese explorers led by Pedro Álvares Cabral, who landed on the shores of what is now Porto Seguro in 1500. The Portuguese were drawn to Brazil by the abundance of natural resources, including timber, precious metals, and fertile land suitable for agriculture. They established a colony and began to exploit the land and its indigenous inhabitants for profit.

In the early years of Portuguese colonization, conflict between the colonizers and indigenous peoples was common as the Portuguese sought to expand their territory and extract resources. However, there were also instances of cooperation and intermarriage between the two groups, leading to the emergence of mixed-race communities known as caboclos.

The Portuguese crown established a system of land grants known as "captaincies" to incentivize settlement and colonization. These captaincies were awarded to nobles and wealthy landowners who were responsible for developing and governing their respective territories. However, many of these captaincies struggled to attract settlers and maintain control over their lands, leading to conflicts and power struggles among the colonists.

In 1549, the Portuguese crown established the Governorate General of Brazil, with its capital at Salvador, in an effort to centralize control over the colony. The arrival of Jesuit missionaries played a significant role in the colonization process, as they sought to convert the indigenous peoples to Christianity and establish missions throughout Brazil.

One of the most significant developments in Brazil's early history was the establishment of sugar plantations along the northeastern coast. The Portuguese brought enslaved Africans to Brazil to work on these plantations, laying the foundation for Brazil's complex and deeply entrenched system of slavery.

Throughout the colonial period, Brazil became a major exporter of sugar, gold, and other commodities, fueling the growth of its economy and attracting settlers from Europe, Africa, and other parts of the world. However, this economic prosperity came at a steep cost, as indigenous peoples were displaced from their lands, enslaved

Africans were subjected to brutal conditions, and the environment was exploited and degraded.

Despite the challenges and injustices of colonization, indigenous peoples and their descendants have persevered, preserving their cultures, languages, and traditions in the face of adversity. Today, Brazil is home to over 300 indigenous ethnic groups, each contributing to the country's rich cultural heritage and diversity.

Portuguese Colonization and the Legacy of Exploration

In the annals of Brazil's history, the era of Portuguese colonization stands as a pivotal chapter, shaping the nation's identity and leaving a lasting legacy of exploration and conquest. The Portuguese were among the first Europeans to set foot on Brazilian soil, spurred by a thirst for adventure, wealth, and imperial expansion. Led by navigators like Pedro Álvares Cabral, who is credited with the discovery of Brazil in 1500, Portuguese explorers embarked on daring voyages across the Atlantic Ocean, charting unknown waters and laying claim to new territories in the name of the Portuguese crown.

The arrival of the Portuguese marked the beginning of a new era for Brazil, as the land and its indigenous inhabitants became enmeshed in the global networks of trade, commerce, and empire. The Portuguese wasted no time in exploiting Brazil's abundant natural resources, establishing settlements, and exploiting the land for its riches. Along the coast, they erected fortified trading posts known as "feitorias" to facilitate the exchange of goods and to protect their interests from rival European powers.

One of the most enduring legacies of Portuguese colonization is the introduction of sugarcane cultivation to Brazil. Recognizing the fertile soil and tropical climate of northeastern Brazil as ideal for sugarcane production, the Portuguese established vast plantations, known as "engenhos," where enslaved Africans toiled under harsh conditions to produce sugar, a highly prized commodity in Europe.

The Portuguese also played a significant role in shaping Brazil's cultural and linguistic identity. They brought with them the Portuguese language, which became the dominant language of Brazil and remains the official language to this day. They also introduced Catholicism, building churches, monasteries, and missions throughout the colony and converting indigenous peoples to Christianity.

Portuguese colonization was not without its challenges and conflicts. Indigenous peoples resisted Portuguese encroachment on their lands, leading to sporadic uprisings and conflicts throughout the colonial period. Additionally, Brazil's vast size and diverse geography presented logistical and administrative challenges for the Portuguese authorities, who struggled to maintain control over their far-flung colonies.

Despite these challenges, Portuguese colonization laid the foundation for Brazil's development as a nation. The influx of European settlers brought new technologies, agricultural practices, and cultural influences to Brazil, contributing to the country's growth and prosperity. However, it also entrenched systems of inequality, exploitation, and oppression that continue to shape Brazilian society to this day.

As we reflect on the legacy of Portuguese colonization, we must reckon with its complexities and contradictions, acknowledging both its achievements and its injustices. The story of Portuguese exploration and conquest in Brazil is a testament to the resilience of indigenous peoples, the endurance of African cultures, and the enduring legacy of colonialism in shaping the modern world.

Independence and the Formation of the Brazilian Nation

The journey toward independence and the formation of the Brazilian nation is a saga marked by upheaval, struggle, and resilience. By the early 19th century, Brazil had been under Portuguese rule for over three centuries, with its vast territory serving as a lucrative colony for the Portuguese crown. However, discontent simmered beneath the surface as Brazilians chafed under colonial exploitation and yearned for greater autonomy and self-determination.

The seeds of independence were sown in 1808 when the Portuguese royal family, fleeing Napoleon's invasion of Portugal, sought refuge in Brazil. The presence of the royal court in Rio de Janeiro brought significant changes to Brazil, including the opening of ports to foreign trade, the establishment of cultural and educational institutions, and the elevation of Brazil to the status of a kingdom within the Portuguese Empire.

As Brazil prospered under royal patronage, calls for independence grew louder. Influenced by Enlightenment ideals of liberty and equality, Brazilian intellectuals and revolutionaries began to agitate for political reform and greater autonomy from Portugal. The movement gained momentum in 1822 when Dom Pedro, the son of the Portuguese king, declared Brazil's independence from Portugal and proclaimed himself emperor.

15

The declaration of independence sparked a period of political turmoil and conflict as rival factions vied for power and influence. Dom Pedro faced opposition from both Portuguese loyalists and republican insurgents, leading to armed uprisings and regional conflicts throughout Brazil. Despite these challenges, Dom Pedro succeeded in consolidating his rule and establishing Brazil as an independent nation.

With independence secured, Brazil embarked on a journey of nation-building and state-building, grappling with the task of forging a cohesive national identity and establishing effective governance structures. Dom Pedro's reign was marked by efforts to modernize Brazil's economy and infrastructure, including the construction of roads, bridges, and railways, and the promotion of industry and commerce.

However, Brazil's transition to independence was not without its setbacks and challenges. The legacy of slavery cast a long shadow over Brazilian society, with millions of enslaved Africans toiling on plantations and in mines, enduring brutal conditions and deprivation of their basic rights. The abolition of slavery in 1888, while a milestone in Brazil's history, did little to address the entrenched inequalities and injustices that continued to plague the country.

Despite these challenges, Brazil emerged from its struggle for independence as a vibrant and dynamic nation, rich in cultural diversity and natural resources. The legacy of independence continues to shape Brazil's identity and trajectory, serving as a testament to the resilience and determination of its people in the face of adversity. As we reflect on Brazil's journey toward nationhood, we must honor the sacrifices of those who fought for freedom and justice and strive to build a more inclusive and equitable society for future generations.

Empire to Republic: Political Transitions and Challenges

The transition from empire to republic marked a significant turning point in Brazil's political history, ushering in a new era of governance, reform, and social change. For much of the 19th century, Brazil was ruled by a monarchy, with Dom Pedro II serving as the country's last emperor. However, discontent with monarchical rule had been brewing for decades, fueled by widespread corruption, economic instability, and calls for political reform.

In 1889, Brazil's long-standing monarchy was overthrown in a bloodless coup d'état, and the country was declared a republic. The transition was met with both hope and uncertainty, as Brazilians grappled with the challenges of building a new political system and forging a sense of national unity in the wake of empire's demise.

The early years of the Brazilian Republic were marked by political turmoil and instability as rival factions vied for power and influence. The new government faced numerous challenges, including economic recession, social unrest, and regional conflicts, as well as pressure from powerful interest groups and foreign powers.

One of the most significant political developments of the early republic was the abolition of slavery in 1888, which brought an end to centuries of forced labor and exploitation. However, the legacy of slavery continued to cast a long shadow over Brazilian society, as former slaves and their descendants struggled to gain access to education, employment, and political representation. The transition to a republic also brought about significant changes in Brazil's political landscape, including the establishment of a federal system of government, with power divided between the central government and the states. The new constitution, adopted in 1891, enshrined principles of democracy, federalism, and individual rights, laying the groundwork for Brazil's modern political system.

However, the promise of democracy was often overshadowed by the realities of Brazilian politics, as the country grappled with issues of corruption, cronyism, and authoritarianism. The early republic was characterized by a series of military coups and dictatorships, as well as periods of civilian rule marked by political patronage and electoral fraud.

Despite these challenges, Brazil made significant strides in economic and social development during the early republic, with the growth of industry, infrastructure, and urbanization transforming the country's economy and society. The influx of immigrants from Europe and Asia brought new skills, ideas, and cultural influences to Brazil, contributing to its rich cultural tapestry and ethnic diversity.

As we reflect on the transition from empire to republic, we must acknowledge both the achievements and the shortcomings of Brazil's political evolution. The story of Brazil's political transitions is one of resilience, adaptability, and perseverance, as the country continues to navigate the complexities of governance and democracy in the 21st century.

Brazil in the 20th Century: From Dictatorship to Democracy

The 20th century was a tumultuous period in Brazil's history, marked by dramatic political upheaval, social change, and economic transformation. Brazil began the century as a young republic, still finding its footing in the wake of the transition from empire to republic in 1889. The early decades of the century were characterized by political instability, as Brazil cycled through a series of civilian and military governments, each grappling with the challenges of governance, economic development, and social reform.

One of the defining moments of Brazil's 20th-century history was the rise of Getúlio Vargas, who came to power in 1930 following a military coup. Vargas' presidency marked a departure from traditional Brazilian politics, as he implemented a series of reforms aimed at modernizing the country's economy and society. During his tenure, Vargas introduced labor laws, social welfare programs, and industrialization initiatives, transforming Brazil into a modern nation-state.

However, Vargas' rule was also marked by authoritarianism and repression, as he cracked down on political dissent and centralized power in his own hands. In 1937, Vargas declared a state of emergency and assumed dictatorial powers, suspending civil liberties and suppressing opposition parties. This period, known as the Estado Novo, lasted until 1945 when Vargas was ousted from power in a coup led by the Brazilian military.

Following Vargas' ouster, Brazil experienced a brief period of democratic rule before another military coup in 1964 ushered in more than two decades of military dictatorship. The military government, led by a series of generals, implemented harsh repression, censorship, and human rights abuses in the name of national security and anticommunism. Despite economic growth and modernization during this period, the military regime faced growing opposition from civil society, including student activists, labor unions, and religious groups.

In the late 1970s, Brazil began a gradual transition to democracy, spurred by a combination of domestic pressure and international condemnation of human rights abuses. In 1985, civilian rule was restored with the election of Tancredo Neves as president, marking the end of military dictatorship and the beginning of a new era of democratic governance in Brazil.

The transition to democracy was not without its challenges, as Brazil grappled with issues of corruption, inequality, and political polarization. However, successive governments have worked to strengthen democratic institutions, expand civil liberties, and promote social inclusion, leading to significant progress in areas such as poverty reduction, education, and healthcare.

Today, Brazil stands as a vibrant democracy, with regular elections, a free press, and a robust civil society. However, the country continues to face challenges, including political corruption, crime, and environmental degradation. As Brazil enters the 21st century, it remains a work in progress, striving to fulfill the promise of democracy and build a better future for all its citizens.

Contemporary Brazil: Socio-Economic Dynamics and Challenges.

In the contemporary landscape of Brazil, a complex interplay of socio-economic dynamics and challenges shapes the nation's trajectory as it navigates the complexities of the modern world. With a population exceeding 200 million people, Brazil is one of the largest and most diverse countries in the world, boasting a rich tapestry of cultures, languages, and traditions. However, beneath the surface of Brazil's vibrant diversity lies a myriad of socio-economic disparities and structural inequalities that present significant challenges to the country's development and well-being.

One of the most pressing challenges facing contemporary Brazil is the issue of income inequality. Despite significant economic growth and progress in recent decades, Brazil remains one of the most unequal countries in the world, with a vast gap between rich and poor. The wealthiest 1% of Brazilians control a disproportionate share of the country's wealth, while millions of Brazilians struggle to make ends meet and access basic services such as healthcare, education, and housing.

Another key challenge facing contemporary Brazil is the persistence of poverty and social exclusion, particularly in marginalized urban areas and rural communities. Millions of Brazilians live in informal settlements known as favelas, where access to basic services such as clean water, sanitation, and electricity is often limited or nonexistent. Poverty is also closely linked to issues such as crime, violence, and substance abuse, exacerbating social tensions and undermining community cohesion.

Brazil's economy is another focal point of contemporary challenges, as the country grapples with issues such as inflation, unemployment, and sluggish growth. Brazil's economy is highly dependent on commodity exports, particularly agricultural products such as soybeans, sugar, and beef, leaving it vulnerable to fluctuations in global commodity prices. Additionally, Brazil faces structural challenges such as inadequate infrastructure, bureaucratic red tape, and an inefficient tax system that hinder productivity and investment.

Environmental sustainability is another critical issue facing contemporary Brazil, as the country grapples with deforestation, pollution, and climate change. The Amazon rainforest, often referred to as the "lungs of the planet," is under threat from logging, mining, and agricultural expansion, leading to widespread environmental degradation and loss of biodiversity. Brazil is also one of the world's largest emitters of greenhouse gases, contributing to global warming and climate instability.

In recent years, Brazil has made significant strides in addressing some of these challenges, including efforts to reduce poverty, expand access to education and healthcare, and promote sustainable development. However, much work remains to be done to ensure that all Brazilians can enjoy the benefits of economic prosperity, social inclusion, and environmental sustainability. As Brazil looks to the future, it must confront these challenges head-on, harnessing the creativity, resilience, and ingenuity of its people to build a more equitable, inclusive, and sustainable society for generations to come.

Natural Wonders: Exploring Brazil's Breathtaking Landscapes

Brazil is a land of extraordinary natural beauty, boasting a diverse array of breathtaking landscapes that captivate the imagination and inspire awe. At the heart of Brazil's natural wonders lies the Amazon rainforest, the largest tropical rainforest on Earth. Covering over 6.7 million square kilometers, the Amazon is a vast and biodiverse ecosystem, home to millions of species of plants, animals, and insects, many of which are found nowhere else on the planet.

In addition to the Amazon, Brazil is blessed with an abundance of other natural wonders, including the Pantanal, the world's largest tropical wetland area. Spanning over 150,000 square kilometers, the Pantanal is a haven for wildlife, teeming with jaguars, caimans, and over 1,000 species of birds. Its seasonal floods create a dynamic landscape of marshes, lagoons, and grasslands, making it one of the most biodiverse habitats on Earth.

Brazil's coastline is another source of natural beauty, with over 7,000 kilometers of sandy beaches, rugged cliffs, and picturesque islands. Along the northeastern coast, visitors will find the stunning sand dunes of Lençóis Maranhenses National Park, where vast expanses of white sand are punctuated by crystal-clear lagoons, creating a surreal and otherworldly landscape.

In the south of Brazil lies the breathtaking Iguazu Falls, one of the most spectacular waterfalls in the world. Spanning the border between Brazil and Argentina, the falls consist of over 275 individual cascades, plunging over towering cliffs into the mist-filled gorge below. Visitors can explore the falls from both Brazilian and Argentinean sides, taking in panoramic views of this natural wonder from a series of walkways and observation points.

Further inland, Brazil is home to a diverse array of landscapes, from the rugged peaks of the Serra da Capivara to the lush valleys of the Atlantic Forest. The Chapada dos Veadeiros National Park, located in the central highlands of Brazil, is known for its stunning waterfalls, crystal-clear rivers, and ancient rock formations, providing a haven for hikers, climbers, and nature lovers alike.

Brazil's natural wonders are not only a source of awe and inspiration but also play a vital role in the country's ecological health and biodiversity. Protecting and preserving these landscapes is essential not only for the well-being of Brazil but for the entire planet. As visitors explore Brazil's breathtaking landscapes, they are reminded of the fragile beauty of our natural world and the importance of conservation and stewardship for future generations.

Amazon Rainforest: Ecological Treasure of the World

The Amazon rainforest stands as one of the most awe-inspiring and ecologically diverse regions on the planet. Spanning over 6.7 million square kilometers across nine South American countries, the Amazon is often referred to as the "lungs of the Earth" due to its crucial role in producing oxygen and regulating the global climate. This vast expanse of greenery is home to an astonishing array of plant and animal species, many of which are found nowhere else on Earth.

The Amazon rainforest is characterized by its dense canopy, towering trees, and intricate network of rivers and tributaries. It is estimated that the Amazon is home to approximately 390 billion individual trees, representing over 16,000 different species. These trees play a vital role in storing carbon dioxide and mitigating climate change, making the Amazon a critical buffer against global warming.

In addition to its impressive flora, the Amazon is also home to an incredible diversity of wildlife, including jaguars, sloths, monkeys, and countless species of birds, insects, and reptiles. It is estimated that the Amazon is home to around 10% of the world's known species, making it one of the most biodiverse regions on Earth. The rivers and waterways of the Amazon are also teeming with life, with thousands of species of fish, amphibians, and aquatic mammals inhabiting its waters.

The Amazon rainforest is not only a biological treasure trove but also a source of invaluable ecosystem services that benefit people around the world. The rainforest helps to regulate the global climate by absorbing carbon dioxide and releasing oxygen through the process of photosynthesis. It also plays a crucial role in regulating rainfall patterns, helping to sustain agriculture, water supplies, and livelihoods for millions of people in South America and beyond.

Despite its ecological importance, the Amazon rainforest is under threat from deforestation, logging, mining, and agricultural expansion. Large swathes of the Amazon have been cleared for cattle ranching, soybean production, and other forms of agriculture, leading to widespread habitat loss, biodiversity loss, and environmental degradation. Deforestation also releases carbon dioxide into the atmosphere, contributing to global warming and climate change.

Efforts to protect and preserve the Amazon rainforest are ongoing, with conservation organizations, governments, and indigenous communities working together to establish protected areas, enforce environmental regulations, and promote sustainable land management practices. However, the challenges facing the Amazon are complex and multifaceted, requiring coordinated action and international cooperation to ensure the long-term health and viability of this vital ecosystem.

As we marvel at the ecological wonders of the Amazon rainforest, we are reminded of the urgent need to safeguard this precious resource for future generations. The fate of the Amazon is intertwined with the fate of the planet, and protecting it is essential for the well-being of all life on Earth.

Wildlife of Brazil: Diverse Fauna in Rich Habitats

The wildlife of Brazil is as diverse and vibrant as the country itself, with an astonishing array of species inhabiting its rich and varied habitats. From the dense rainforests of the Amazon to the vast wetlands of the Pantanal, Brazil is home to an incredible diversity of fauna, including mammals, birds, reptiles, amphibians, and insects.

In the Amazon rainforest, jaguars reign supreme as the apex predators, stalking the forest floor in search of prey. These magnificent big cats are joined by other iconic species such as sloths, tapirs, and giant anteaters, each adapted to their unique role in this complex ecosystem. High in the canopy, troops of monkeys swing through the trees, while colorful birds flit among the branches, filling the air with their calls and songs.

In the Pantanal, the world's largest tropical wetland area, visitors can encounter an abundance of wildlife, from caimans and capybaras to giant otters and hyacinth macaws. The Pantanal is a haven for birdwatchers, with over 650 species of birds recorded in the region, including toucans, herons, and jabirus. During the wet season, when much of the Pantanal is submerged underwater, visitors can witness the spectacle of wildlife congregating on elevated islands of dry land, creating a stunning display of biodiversity.

Brazil's Atlantic Forest, although greatly diminished by deforestation, still harbors a wealth of biodiversity, including endangered species such as the golden lion tamarin and the red-bellied tree frog. Along the coast, visitors can observe sea turtles nesting on remote beaches, while offshore, coral reefs teem with colorful marine life, including reef fish, sharks, and dolphins.

In the Cerrado, Brazil's savanna region, visitors can encounter a unique assemblage of wildlife adapted to the harsh conditions of this arid landscape. Armadillos, anteaters, and giant anteaters roam the grasslands in search of food, while birds of prey soar overhead in search of prey. The Cerrado is also home to a rich diversity of plant species, many of which are found nowhere else on Earth.

Throughout Brazil, efforts are underway to protect and preserve its rich biodiversity, from establishing national parks and protected areas to promoting sustainable land management practices. However, the challenges facing Brazil's wildlife are complex and multifaceted, including habitat loss, deforestation, poaching, and climate change. As we marvel at the incredible diversity of wildlife in Brazil, we are reminded of the importance of conservation and stewardship in ensuring the survival of these precious species for future generations.

Gastronomic Delights: A Journey Through Brazilian Cuisine

Embark on a culinary journey through the vibrant and diverse flavors of Brazilian cuisine, where a rich tapestry of cultural influences and regional ingredients come together to create a feast for the senses. From the lush rainforests of the Amazon to the sun-drenched shores of the Atlantic coast, Brazil's culinary landscape is as varied and vibrant as its people and geography.

At the heart of Brazilian cuisine is the tradition of churrasco, or Brazilian barbecue, a feast of grilled meats that originated in the southern region of the country. In churrascarias, or barbecue restaurants, diners are treated to a smorgasbord of skewered meats, including succulent cuts of beef, pork, chicken, and lamb, slow-roasted over an open flame and seasoned with salt and spices. Accompanying the meats are an array of side dishes, such as farofa (toasted cassava flour), pão de queijo (cheese bread), and feijoada (a hearty stew of beans and pork).

Seafood also plays a prominent role in Brazilian cuisine, thanks to the country's extensive coastline and abundant marine resources. Along the coast, visitors can sample fresh-caught fish, shrimp, lobster, and crab, prepared in a variety of ways, from grilled and fried to stewed and steamed. Moqueca, a traditional Brazilian seafood stew made with fish, coconut milk, tomatoes, and spices, is a beloved dish that hails from the northeastern state of Bahia.

33

In the Amazon region, indigenous ingredients such as fruits, nuts, and exotic meats take center stage in traditional dishes like tacacá, a spicy soup made with tucupi (a fermented manioc broth), jambu (a leafy green vegetable), and dried shrimp. Another Amazonian specialty is pirarucu, a giant freshwater fish that is often grilled or fried and served with a side of farofa and vinaigrette.

No journey through Brazilian cuisine would be complete without sampling the country's famous street food offerings. In cities like Rio de Janeiro and São Paulo, vendors hawk a dizzying array of snacks and treats, from pastel (deep-fried pastries filled with meat, cheese, or shrimp) to coxinha (deep-fried dough stuffed with shredded chicken) to acarajé (deep-fried balls of black-eyed pea dough filled with shrimp and spicy sauce).

To wash it all down, why not indulge in a refreshing caipirinha, Brazil's national cocktail made with cachaça (a distilled spirit made from sugarcane), lime, sugar, and ice? Or perhaps a cold glass of açaí, a purple-hued superfood smoothie made from the berries of the açaí palm tree, native to the Amazon rainforest?

Whether you're a meat lover, a seafood aficionado, or simply have a sweet tooth, Brazilian cuisine offers something for everyone. So grab a plate, pull up a chair, and get ready to savor the flavors of Brazil, where every meal is a celebration of culture, tradition, and culinary craftsmanship.

Feijoada to Brigadeiro: Iconic Brazilian Dishes and Desserts

Explore the vibrant tapestry of Brazilian cuisine, where every dish tells a story of cultural heritage, culinary tradition, and regional flavors. At the heart of Brazil's gastronomic identity lies feijoada, a hearty stew of black beans, pork, and beef that is often considered the country's national dish. Originating in the state of Rio de Janeiro, feijoada is traditionally enjoyed on Saturdays, when families and friends gather to savor this rich and flavorful meal. Accompanying the feijoada are an array of side dishes, including rice, collard greens, farofa (toasted cassava flour), and orange slices, all served together to create a symphony of flavors and textures.

Another iconic Brazilian dish is moqueca, a flavorful seafood stew that hails from the northeastern state of Bahia. Made with fish, shrimp, or other seafood, and simmered in a fragrant broth of coconut milk, tomatoes, onions, peppers, and spices, moqueca is a celebration of Brazil's coastal bounty. Served with a side of rice and farofa, moqueca is a comforting and satisfying meal that captures the essence of Brazilian cuisine.

No culinary tour of Brazil would be complete without indulging in brigadeiro, a beloved Brazilian dessert that is enjoyed by people of all ages. Made with just three ingredients—condensed milk, cocoa powder, and butter—brigadeiro is a simple yet decadent treat that is rolled into bite-sized balls and coated in chocolate sprinkles. Often served at birthday parties, weddings, and other celebrations, brigadeiro is a sweet reminder of the joy and camaraderie that food can bring.

Another popular Brazilian dessert is açaí na tigela, a refreshing and nutritious smoothie bowl made from frozen açaí berries blended with banana and other fruits, and topped with granola, honey, and sliced fruit. Originating in the Amazon region, açaí na tigela has become a favorite snack and breakfast dish across Brazil, thanks to its delicious flavor and health benefits.

For those with a sweet tooth, be sure to sample paçoca, a traditional Brazilian candy made from ground peanuts, sugar, and salt, pressed into a dense and chewy block. Paçoca is a popular treat during festivals and holidays, and is often enjoyed with a cup of coffee or a glass of cachaça, Brazil's national spirit.

Whether you're savoring the rich flavors of feijoada, indulging in the sweet delights of brigadeiro, or cooling off with a refreshing bowl of açaí na tigela, Brazilian cuisine offers a feast for the senses that is sure to leave a lasting impression. So pull up a chair, grab a fork, and get ready to embark on a culinary journey through the flavors of Brazil, where every bite is a celebration of culture, tradition, and good food.

Samba, Carnaval, and Capoeira: Cultural Expressions of Brazil

Brazil's cultural landscape is a vibrant tapestry woven with the threads of samba, Carnaval, and capoeira—expressions that reflect the country's rich history, diverse heritage, and dynamic spirit. At the heart of Brazilian culture is samba, a lively and infectious musical genre that originated in the Afro-Brazilian communities of Rio de Janeiro in the late 19th century. Rooted in African rhythms and traditions, samba is characterized by its syncopated beats, pulsating percussion, and energetic dance movements. Today, samba is celebrated throughout Brazil and beyond, with elaborate samba schools competing in the annual Carnaval parades and samba clubs hosting regular dance parties known as "rodas de samba."

Speaking of Carnaval, this iconic festival is the ultimate expression of Brazilian culture, bringing together millions of revelers from across the country and around the world for days of music, dance, and celebration. Dating back to the colonial era, Carnaval is a time-honored tradition that takes place in the weeks leading up to Lent, with festivities reaching a fever pitch in cities like Rio de Janeiro, Salvador, and Recife. The highlight of Carnaval is the samba parades, where elaborately costumed dancers, musicians, and floats parade through the streets in a dazzling display of color, rhythm, and pageantry. In addition to the parades, Carnaval also features street parties, live concerts, and cultural events, making it one of the largest and most spectacular festivals in the world.

Another cultural expression synonymous with Brazil is capoeira, a unique martial art that combines elements of dance, acrobatics, and music. Originating in the Afro-Brazilian communities of the colonial era, capoeira was developed as a form of self-defense and resistance against oppression. Today, capoeira is practiced by millions of people around the world, with schools and academies teaching the art of capoeira in countries as far-flung as Japan, Australia, and the United States. Central to the practice of capoeira is the roda, or circle, where practitioners gather to play music, sing songs, and engage in friendly sparring matches known as "jogos." The music of capoeira, played on traditional instruments such as the berimbau, pandeiro, and atabaque, sets the rhythm and pace of the game, while the movements of the players—fluid and graceful, yet powerful and precise—reflect the dynamic interplay of combat and dance.

In addition to samba, Carnaval, and capoeira, Brazil is also renowned for its rich culinary traditions, vibrant visual arts scene, and diverse religious practices, all of which contribute to the country's unique cultural identity. Whether you're dancing to the rhythm of the samba drums, parading through the streets in a glittering Carnaval costume, or playing capoeira in the roda, Brazil offers a kaleidoscope of cultural experiences that are as diverse and dynamic as the country itself.

Religion and Spirituality: Diversity in Faith and Practice

Religion and spirituality hold a prominent place in the cultural fabric of Brazil, where a diverse tapestry of faiths and practices coexist harmoniously, reflecting the country's rich history of colonization, immigration, and cultural exchange. At the heart of Brazil's religious landscape is Christianity, with the majority of Brazilians identifying as Catholic. Catholicism was introduced to Brazil by Portuguese colonizers in the 16th century and remains the dominant religion in the country, with millions of Brazilians adhering to the teachings and traditions of the Catholic Church. Brazilian Catholicism is characterized by a blend of European Catholicism, indigenous beliefs, and African spiritual practices, resulting in a unique syncretic religion that incorporates elements of all three traditions.

In addition to Catholicism, Brazil is also home to a significant Protestant population, with millions of Brazilians belonging to Protestant denominations such as Pentecostalism, Evangelicalism, and Baptist. Protestantism has experienced rapid growth in Brazil in recent decades, particularly among urban and marginalized communities, thanks to its emphasis on personal salvation, spiritual renewal, and community empowerment.

Alongside Christianity, Brazil is also home to a diverse array of Afro-Brazilian religions, which synthesize elements of African spiritual traditions with Catholicism and indigenous beliefs. The most prominent of these Afro-Brazilian religions is Candomblé, which originated among enslaved Africans brought to Brazil during the colonial era. Candomblé is characterized by its worship of orixás, or deities, who are believed to embody the forces of nature and govern the affairs of human life. Another Afro-Brazilian religion is Umbanda, which emerged in the early 20th century and incorporates elements of spiritism, indigenous shamanism, and Catholicism.

In addition to these major religious traditions, Brazil is also home to a diverse array of indigenous beliefs and practices, with hundreds of indigenous tribes practicing their own unique forms of spirituality and religion. These indigenous traditions are deeply rooted in the land, the natural world, and the cycles of life and death, with rituals and ceremonies often centered around hunting, farming, and seasonal changes.

As Brazil continues to evolve and modernize, its religious landscape remains dynamic and fluid, with new forms of spirituality emerging alongside traditional beliefs and practices. Despite the diversity of faiths and practices, religion continues to play a central role in the lives of millions of Brazilians, providing a sense of community, belonging, and meaning in an ever-changing world.

Language and Communication: Portuguese in Brazilian Context

Language and communication are fundamental aspects of Brazilian culture, with Portuguese serving as the country's official language and primary means of communication. Introduced to Brazil by Portuguese colonizers in the 16th century, Portuguese has evolved over time to become uniquely Brazilian, with its own regional dialects, accents, and colloquialisms. Brazilian Portuguese differs from European Portuguese in pronunciation, vocabulary, and grammar, reflecting the country's diverse cultural heritage and linguistic influences.

One of the defining features of Brazilian Portuguese is its rhythmic and melodic cadence, characterized by nasal vowels, vowel reduction, and a sing-song intonation pattern. Brazilians are known for their expressive and animated style of communication, often using gestures, facial expressions, and body language to convey meaning and emotion. This expressive communication style is reflected in the Portuguese language itself, with words and phrases often infused with colorful metaphors, idioms, and slang.

Brazilian Portuguese is a dynamic and ever-evolving language, constantly adapting to new cultural, technological, and social influences. In recent decades, for example, English loanwords and expressions have become increasingly common in Brazilian Portuguese, particularly in the fields of technology, business, and pop culture. Similarly, indigenous languages and African languages have left their mark on Brazilian Portuguese, with words and phrases from languages such as Tupi-Guarani and Yoruba enriching the country's linguistic landscape.

In addition to Portuguese, Brazil is also home to a rich tapestry of indigenous languages, with over 200 different languages spoken by indigenous communities across the country. Many of these indigenous languages are endangered, threatened by the encroachment of Portuguese and the erosion of traditional ways of life. Efforts are underway to preserve and revitalize indigenous languages in Brazil, including initiatives to promote bilingual education, linguistic research, and cultural revitalization programs.

In contemporary Brazil, Portuguese is the language of government, education, media, and business, serving as a unifying force in a country characterized by its vast size and cultural diversity. While Portuguese is the dominant language in Brazil, the country's linguistic landscape is also enriched by the presence of immigrant communities who speak languages such as Italian, German, Japanese, and Arabic, adding further layers of linguistic diversity to Brazilian society.

Overall, language and communication play a central role in shaping Brazilian identity and culture, serving as a bridge between the country's past and present, its diverse peoples and regions, and its rich tapestry of traditions and experiences. As Brazil continues to evolve and grow, so too will its language and communication practices, reflecting the country's ongoing journey of cultural and linguistic transformation.

Brazilian Music: A Melting Pot of Rhythms and Styles

Brazilian music is a vibrant and diverse tapestry of rhythms, styles, and influences that reflects the country's rich cultural heritage and multicultural roots. From the infectious beats of samba to the soulful melodies of bossa nova, Brazilian music encompasses a wide range of genres and traditions, each with its own unique flavor and character.

At the heart of Brazilian music is samba, a lively and rhythmic genre that originated in the Afro-Brazilian communities of Rio de Janeiro in the late 19th century. Characterized by its syncopated rhythms, pulsating percussion, and infectious dance moves, samba is the sound of Carnival and the soul of Brazil. From the raucous street parties of Rio's favelas to the elegant ballrooms of Copacabana, samba is the soundtrack of Brazilian life, bringing people together in celebration and joy.

Another iconic Brazilian music genre is bossa nova, a laid-back and sophisticated style that emerged in the late 1950s and quickly gained international acclaim. Combining elements of samba, jazz, and classical music, bossa nova is characterized by its smooth melodies, gentle rhythms, and intimate vocals. Artists such as João Gilberto, Antonio Carlos Jobim, and Astrud Gilberto helped to popularize bossa nova around the world, with songs like "The Girl from Ipanema" becoming timeless classics.

In addition to samba and bossa nova, Brazil is also home to a wealth of other musical genres and traditions, including forró, axé, maracatu, frevo, and choro, each with its own regional variations and cultural significance. Forró, for example, originated in the northeast of Brazil and is characterized by its lively accordion-driven rhythms and energetic dance moves. Axé, on the other hand, emerged in the state of Bahia and is known for its infectious beats, catchy melodies, and colorful Carnival celebrations.

Brazilian music is also influenced by a rich tapestry of cultural traditions, including indigenous, African, European, and indigenous influences. The rhythms of African drumming, the melodies of Portuguese fado, and the harmonies of indigenous chants all contribute to the vibrant mosaic of Brazilian music, creating a sound that is uniquely Brazilian yet deeply rooted in global musical traditions.

Today, Brazilian music continues to evolve and thrive, with artists experimenting with new sounds, styles, and technologies to push the boundaries of creativity and innovation. From the bustling streets of São Paulo to the remote villages of the Amazon rainforest, music is an integral part of Brazilian life, weaving its way through the fabric of everyday existence and connecting people across cultures, generations, and geography.

Literature and Arts: Influential Voices and Creative Expression

Literature and the arts hold a special place in the cultural tapestry of Brazil, serving as a reflection of the country's complex history, diverse society, and rich cultural heritage. From the literary works of Machado de Assis to the vibrant paintings of Tarsila do Amaral, Brazilian artists and writers have made significant contributions to the global artistic landscape, inspiring audiences around the world with their creativity, innovation, and passion.

One of the most influential figures in Brazilian literature is Machado de Assis, often regarded as the greatest writer in Brazilian history. Born in Rio de Janeiro in 1839, Machado de Assis rose from humble beginnings to become a literary giant, known for his incisive wit, keen insight into human nature, and groundbreaking narrative techniques. His novels, including "Dom Casmurro" and "The Posthumous Memoirs of Brás Cubas," are celebrated for their psychological depth, social commentary, and timeless relevance, making Machado de Assis a towering figure in Brazilian literature.

In addition to Machado de Assis, Brazil has produced a wealth of other literary luminaries, including Clarice Lispector, Jorge Amado, and Carlos Drummond de Andrade, each of whom has left an indelible mark on the literary landscape of Brazil and beyond. Clarice Lispector, with her enigmatic prose and introspective style, is often hailed as one of the greatest writers of the 20th century, while Jorge Amado, with his colorful characters and vivid storytelling, captured the spirit of

Brazil's northeastern region in works such as "Dona Flor and Her Two Husbands."

Brazilian literature is as diverse as the country itself, encompassing a wide range of themes, styles, and genres, from magical realism to social realism, from poetry to prose. Writers like João Guimarães Rosa, with his experimental language and inventive storytelling, have pushed the boundaries of literary expression, while poets like Vinicius de Moraes and Carlos Drummond de Andrade have captured the beauty and complexity of Brazilian life in verse.

In addition to literature, Brazil is also home to a vibrant and dynamic arts scene, with artists working in a variety of mediums, including painting, sculpture, photography, and performance art. Tarsila do Amaral, with her bold colors and geometric shapes, is considered one of the pioneers of modern art in Brazil, while artists like Candido Portinari and Emiliano Di Cavalcanti have left their mark on Brazilian art with their powerful depictions of social and political themes.

From the streets of Rio de Janeiro to the galleries of São Paulo, Brazilian artists and writers continue to inspire and challenge audiences with their creativity, innovation, and passion for their craft. Whether exploring the complexities of Brazilian identity, confronting social injustices, or celebrating the beauty of everyday life, literature and the arts play a vital role in shaping the cultural identity of Brazil and its people.

Carnival: Festive Traditions and Spectacular Celebrations

Carnival is the ultimate celebration of joy, music, and culture in Brazil, captivating millions of people from around the world with its vibrant colors, infectious rhythms, and electrifying energy. Rooted in centuries-old traditions of pre-Lenten festivities, Carnival is a time for revelry, revelry, and revelry. It takes place in the weeks leading up to Lent, culminating in a whirlwind of parades, parties, and performances that transform cities and towns across Brazil into a kaleidoscope of sights and sounds.

The origins of Carnival in Brazil can be traced back to the colonial era when Portuguese settlers brought the tradition of pre-Lenten celebrations to the shores of Brazil. Over time, these celebrations evolved to incorporate elements of African and indigenous cultures, resulting in the unique and vibrant Carnival we know today. The festivities are characterized by elaborate costumes, extravagant floats, and exuberant street parties, with participants dancing to the rhythm of samba music and savoring the spirit of camaraderie and community.

The heart of Carnival beats strongest in Rio de Janeiro, home to the world-famous samba parades of the Sambadrome. Here, samba schools from across the city compete in a dazzling display of creativity and showmanship, with each school vying for the coveted title of Carnival champion. Months of preparation go into designing costumes, choreographing dances, and constructing floats, as samba schools pull out all the stops to impress judges and spectators alike.

But Carnival is not just about the Sambadrome—it's also about the street parties, known as blocos, that take place throughout the city. These blocos attract revelers of all ages, backgrounds, and walks of life, who come together to dance, sing, and celebrate in the streets. From the traditional Banda de Ipanema to the hipster-friendly Sargento Pimenta, there is a bloco for everyone, each with its own unique vibe and atmosphere.

Beyond Rio de Janeiro, Carnival is celebrated in cities and towns across Brazil, from Salvador to Recife to São Paulo. Each region puts its own spin on the festivities, incorporating local traditions, music, and culture into the Carnival experience. In Salvador, for example, Carnival is known for its trio elétrico trucks, which parade through the streets blasting music and carrying performers atop towering platforms. In Recife, Carnival is celebrated with frevo, a fast-paced dance style accompanied by brass bands and colorful umbrellas.

But no matter where you go in Brazil during Carnival, one thing is certain: you'll be swept up in the spirit of the festivities, as the country comes alive with music, dance, and revelry. It's a time to let loose, forget your worries, and immerse yourself in the magic of Carnival, where the streets pulse with energy and the air is filled with the sounds of celebration.

Soccer Nation: The Passion and Legacy of Futebol

In Brazil, soccer isn't just a sport—it's a way of life, a national obsession, and a source of pride and passion for millions of people across the country. From the bustling streets of Rio de Janeiro to the remote villages of the Amazon rainforest, soccer is woven into the fabric of Brazilian culture, shaping identities, forging communities, and fueling dreams of glory on the world stage.

The roots of soccer in Brazil can be traced back to the late 19th century when British expatriates introduced the sport to the country. Since then, soccer has grown to become the most popular sport in Brazil, with millions of Brazilians of all ages and backgrounds playing and following the game with unwavering devotion.

One of the defining characteristics of Brazilian soccer is its distinctive style of play, known for its creativity, flair, and attacking prowess. Brazilian players are celebrated for their skillful dribbling, precise passing, and dazzling footwork, with legends like Pelé, Zico, and Ronaldo inspiring generations of players with their artistry and athleticism.

At the heart of Brazilian soccer is the seleção brasileira, the national team, which has achieved unparalleled success on the international stage, winning the FIFA World Cup a record five times. The seleção's triumphs in 1958, 1962, 1970, 1994, and 2002 have cemented Brazil's reputation as a soccer powerhouse and earned the team a legion of fans around the world. But soccer in Brazil is about more than just winning—it's about the passion, the pageantry, and the sense of belonging that comes from supporting your team through thick and thin. From the raucous chants of torcidas (soccer fan groups) to the colorful displays of banners and flags in stadiums, soccer matches in Brazil are a spectacle like no other, where the energy and excitement of the crowd can be felt from miles away.

In addition to the national team, Brazil is also home to a rich tapestry of club soccer, with teams like Flamengo, Corinthians, and São Paulo boasting large and passionate fan bases. Matches between rival clubs are fiercely contested affairs, with bragging rights and local pride on the line.

But perhaps the most enduring legacy of soccer in Brazil is its impact on society, serving as a vehicle for social change, empowerment, and opportunity. Soccer has the power to unite people from different backgrounds and walks of life, breaking down barriers and fostering a sense of solidarity and camaraderie. For many young Brazilians, soccer offers a pathway out of poverty and a chance to pursue their dreams on and off the field.

In Brazil, soccer isn't just a game—it's a way of life, a source of joy and inspiration, and a symbol of national identity. Whether playing in the streets, cheering in the stands, or watching on television, soccer is a shared passion that brings people together and transcends boundaries, reminding us of the power of sport to uplift, inspire, and unite.

Rio de Janeiro: Iconic City of Contrasts and Charm

Rio de Janeiro, often referred to as the "Cidade Maravilhosa" or Marvelous City, is a vibrant metropolis nestled between lush mountains and sparkling beaches on Brazil's southeastern coast. With its iconic landmarks, colorful neighborhoods, and lively culture, Rio de Janeiro captivates visitors from around the world with its unique blend of contrasts and charm.

At the heart of Rio de Janeiro lies its most famous attraction, the Christ the Redeemer statue, standing tall atop Corcovado Mountain. This towering monument, with its outstretched arms and panoramic views of the city below, has become an enduring symbol of Rio and a must-visit destination for tourists and pilgrims alike.

But Rio's allure extends far beyond Christ the Redeemer, with a wealth of other attractions waiting to be discovered. Copacabana Beach, with its golden sands and bustling promenade, is a playground for sun-seekers and beachgoers, while nearby Ipanema Beach beckons with its laid-back vibe and world-class surfing. From the historic streets of downtown Rio to the bohemian charm of Santa Teresa, the city's neighborhoods offer a diverse array of experiences, each with its own unique character and charm.

One of the highlights of Rio de Janeiro is its vibrant street life, where music, dance, and celebration spill out into the streets day and night. Whether it's the pulsating rhythms of samba at a local bar or the colorful costumes and infectious energy of a Carnival parade, Rio's streets are alive with the sounds and sights of Brazilian culture.

Of course, no visit to Rio de Janeiro would be complete without experiencing the thrill of Carnival, the world's largest and most spectacular festival. For five days leading up to Lent, the city erupts in a frenzy of music, dance, and revelry, as millions of people take to the streets to celebrate in a riot of color and sound. The Sambadrome, with its elaborate parades and dazzling costumes, is the epicenter of Carnival, but the festivities extend throughout the city, with blocos (street parties) and balls happening in every neighborhood.

But amid the glitz and glamour of Rio de Janeiro lies a city of contrasts, where luxury high-rises overlook sprawling favelas and opulent mansions stand side by side with makeshift shacks. The city's social inequalities are stark, with pockets of poverty and wealth existing side by side, creating a complex and often contradictory urban landscape.

Despite its challenges, Rio de Janeiro remains a city of undeniable charm and beauty, where the warmth and hospitality of its people shine through even in the face of adversity. Whether exploring its iconic landmarks, soaking up the sun on its beaches, or immersing yourself in its vibrant culture, Rio de Janeiro offers a truly unforgettable experience that will leave you enchanted and inspired.

São Paulo: Brazil's Economic and Cultural Hub

São Paulo, the sprawling metropolis of Brazil's southeast, stands as the economic and cultural powerhouse of the nation. With its towering skyscrapers, bustling streets, and vibrant cultural scene, São Paulo is a city of contrasts and contradictions, where tradition meets modernity, and old-world charm coexists with cutting-edge innovation.

As the largest city in Brazil and the economic heart of South America, São Paulo is a magnet for business, industry, and commerce. Home to the São Paulo Stock Exchange and the headquarters of many multinational corporations, including banks, tech companies, and pharmaceutical giants, São Paulo drives Brazil's economy forward, generating wealth and opportunity for millions of people.

But São Paulo is more than just a center of finance and industry—it's also a melting pot of cultures, languages, and traditions, with a rich tapestry of diversity that reflects Brazil's complex history of immigration and settlement. From the Italian immigrants who brought pizza and pasta to the city in the early 20th century to the Japanese immigrants who established São Paulo's vibrant Liberdade neighborhood, São Paulo's cultural heritage is as diverse as its population.

One of the defining features of São Paulo is its dynamic arts and entertainment scene, with world-class museums, theaters, and galleries showcasing the best of Brazilian and international culture. The São Paulo Museum of Art (MASP), with its iconic red suspended structure, is home to an impressive collection of European and Brazilian art, while institutions like the São Paulo Biennial and the São Paulo International Film Festival attract artists and filmmakers from around the globe.

São Paulo's culinary scene is equally renowned, with a wealth of restaurants, cafes, and food markets serving up a tantalizing array of flavors and cuisines. From traditional Brazilian dishes like feijoada and coxinha to international fare like sushi and falafel, São Paulo's dining options cater to every taste and budget, making it a paradise for food lovers.

But amid São Paulo's glitz and glamour lies a city of contrasts, where luxury condos overlook sprawling favelas and gleaming skyscrapers cast shadows over crowded streets. The city's social inequalities are stark, with pockets of wealth and poverty existing side by side, creating a complex urban landscape that is both awe-inspiring and heartbreaking.

Despite its challenges, São Paulo remains a city of opportunity and possibility, where people from all walks of life come together to pursue their dreams and build a better future. Whether exploring its vibrant neighborhoods, soaking up its cultural offerings, or sampling its culinary delights, São Paulo offers a truly unforgettable experience that will leave you inspired and amazed.

Brasília: Modernist Architecture and Political Center

Brasília, the capital of Brazil, is a city unlike any other, known for its bold modernist architecture and status as the political center of the country. Designed by the visionary architect Oscar Niemeyer and urban planner Lúcio Costa, Brasília was built from scratch in the late 1950s to fulfill the vision of then-President Juscelino Kubitschek, who sought to create a modern, efficient capital that would symbolize Brazil's aspirations for the future.

At the heart of Brasília lies the Plano Piloto, the city's central area, which is laid out in the shape of an airplane and organized into distinct sectors designated for different functions, such as government, commerce, and residential areas. The most iconic buildings in Brasília are located in the Monumental Axis, including the National Congress, designed by Oscar Niemeyer, with its twin towers and striking dome, and the Palácio da Alvorada, the official residence of the President of Brazil, known for its sleek, minimalist design and serene lakeside setting.

But Brasília's architectural marvels extend beyond the Monumental Axis, with numerous other landmarks and structures that showcase the city's commitment to modernism and innovation. The Cathedral of Brasília, with its hyperboloid structure and stained glass windows, is a masterpiece of contemporary architecture and a symbol of faith and spirituality in the heart of the city. The Brasília TV Tower, standing over 220 meters tall, offers panoramic views of the city and surrounding landscape, while the Cultural

Complex of the Republic houses museums, theaters, and galleries dedicated to showcasing Brazilian culture and heritage.

In addition to its architectural significance, Brasília is also the political center of Brazil, serving as the seat of the federal government and home to the executive, legislative, and judicial branches. The Palácio do Planalto, which houses the offices of the President, and the Supreme Federal Court are among the many government buildings located in Brasília, symbolizing the city's importance as the administrative hub of the nation.

But Brasília is more than just a city of government and architecture—it's also a vibrant and dynamic cultural center, with a thriving arts scene, lively music scene, and diverse culinary offerings. From world-class museums and galleries to bustling markets and street vendors, Brasília offers something for everyone, whether you're a history buff, art enthusiast, or foodie.

Despite its relatively short history, Brasília has quickly become one of Brazil's most important and influential cities, serving as a symbol of progress, modernity, and national identity. With its bold architecture, political significance, and cultural vibrancy, Brasília continues to inspire and captivate visitors from around the world, inviting them to experience the unique spirit and energy of Brazil's capital city.

Salvador: Afro-Brazilian Heritage and Vibrant Culture

Salvador, the capital of the northeastern state of Bahia, is a city steeped in history, culture, and Afro-Brazilian heritage. Founded in 1549 by the Portuguese as the first capital of Brazil, Salvador played a central role in the country's colonial past and served as a major hub for the transatlantic slave trade. Today, Salvador is renowned for its vibrant culture, colorful festivals, and rich blend of African, indigenous, and European influences.

One of the most striking aspects of Salvador is its Afro-Brazilian heritage, which is deeply ingrained in the city's culture, music, and religion. The majority of Salvador's population is of African descent, with many residents tracing their roots back to the enslaved Africans brought to Brazil during the colonial era. This African influence is evident in Salvador's music, dance, and cuisine, as well as in its religious practices, with traditions such as Candomblé and Capoeira playing a central role in the city's cultural identity.

Salvador is famous for its vibrant music scene, with rhythms such as samba, reggae, and axé permeating the streets and squares of the city. The Pelourinho neighborhood, with its cobblestone streets and colorful colonial buildings, is a UNESCO World Heritage Site and a center of musical and cultural activity, hosting live performances, street parties, and festivals throughout the year.

One of the most iconic symbols of Salvador is the Elevador Lacerda, a historic elevator that connects the lower and upper parts of the city. Built in 1873, the Elevador Lacerda offers panoramic views of Salvador's picturesque coastline and is a popular tourist attraction.

Salvador is also known for its vibrant Carnival celebrations, which rival those of Rio de Janeiro in scale and spectacle. The city's Carnival festivities are a riot of color, music, and dance, with parades, blocos, and street parties taking place throughout the city. Salvador's Carnival is particularly renowned for its trio elétrico trucks, which roam the streets blasting music and carrying revelers in a sea of excitement and energy.

In addition to its cultural attractions, Salvador is home to a wealth of historical landmarks and architectural treasures. The Pelourinho neighborhood is dotted with colonial churches, museums, and palaces, while the Mercado Modelo offers a glimpse into Salvador's bustling market scene, with vendors selling everything from local handicrafts to fresh seafood.

But perhaps the most enduring legacy of Salvador is its warm and welcoming spirit, with residents known for their hospitality, friendliness, and joie de vivre. Whether exploring the city's historic landmarks, soaking up its vibrant culture, or simply relaxing on its sun-kissed beaches, visitors to Salvador are sure to be enchanted by the city's unique blend of history, heritage, and charm.

Recife and Olinda: Colonial Charms and Coastal Beauty

Recife and Olinda, two neighboring cities in the northeastern state of Pernambuco, are renowned for their colonial charms, rich history, and stunning coastal beauty. Situated along the shores of the Atlantic Ocean, these sister cities offer visitors a glimpse into Brazil's colonial past, with their well-preserved historic districts, charming cobblestone streets, and centuries-old architecture.

Recife, often referred to as the "Venice of Brazil" due to its intricate network of canals, is the capital and largest city of Pernambuco. Founded by the Portuguese in the early 16th century, Recife quickly grew into a bustling port city and became a center of trade and commerce during Brazil's colonial period. Today, Recife is a vibrant metropolis known for its cultural diversity, lively music scene, and thriving arts community.

One of the highlights of Recife is its historic district of Recife Antigo, where visitors can wander through narrow alleyways lined with colorful colonial buildings, visit historic churches and museums, and soak up the city's unique atmosphere. The Marco Zero square, located in the heart of Recife Antigo, is a popular gathering spot and offers stunning views of the nearby harbor.

Just a short drive from Recife lies the picturesque town of Olinda, a UNESCO World Heritage Site known for its well-preserved colonial architecture and

59

breathtaking vistas. Founded in the 16th century by the Portuguese, Olinda was once the capital of Pernambuco and served as an important center of culture, religion, and commerce. Today, Olinda is a charming and laid-back destination, with its cobblestone streets, colorful colonial houses, and lush gardens attracting visitors from near and far.

One of the most iconic features of Olinda is its historic churches and convents, many of which date back to the colonial era. The São Bento Monastery, with its ornate baroque architecture and gilded altars, is a masterpiece of colonial craftsmanship and a must-visit destination for history and architecture enthusiasts. The Church of São Francisco, adorned with intricate azulejo tiles and elaborate carvings, is another architectural gem that showcases the rich cultural heritage of Olinda.

In addition to its historic landmarks, Olinda is also known for its lively cultural scene, with festivals, art galleries, and street performances happening throughout the year. The annual Carnival celebrations in Olinda are among the most famous in Brazil, with colorful parades, music, and dancing taking over the streets of the city for days on end.

But perhaps the most captivating aspect of Recife and Olinda is their stunning coastal beauty, with miles of sandy beaches, crystal-clear waters, and swaying palm trees stretching along the Atlantic coast. Whether relaxing on the beach, exploring the historic streets, or immersing yourself in the local culture, Recife and Olinda offer a truly unforgettable experience that will leave you enchanted and inspired.

Manaus: Gateway to the Amazon and Urban Jungle

Manaus, located in the heart of the Amazon rainforest, serves as the gateway to one of the most biodiverse and ecologically significant regions on the planet. Situated at the confluence of the Rio Negro and Solimões rivers, Manaus is the largest city in the Brazilian Amazon and a bustling metropolis surrounded by dense jungle and waterways teeming with life.

Originally founded as a Portuguese fort in the 17th century, Manaus flourished during the rubber boom of the late 19th and early 20th centuries, when the city became one of the wealthiest and most important rubber-producing centers in the world. The wealth generated by the rubber trade led to the construction of opulent palaces, theaters, and mansions, earning Manaus the nickname "Paris of the Tropics" and leaving behind a legacy of grand architecture and cultural richness.

One of the most iconic landmarks in Manaus is the Teatro Amazonas, a magnificent opera house built during the height of the rubber boom. With its stunning neoclassical façade, ornate interiors, and world-class performances, the Teatro Amazonas is a testament to the city's golden age of prosperity and remains a cultural symbol of Manaus to this day.

But despite its urban development, Manaus is surrounded by the vast wilderness of the Amazon rainforest, which stretches for thousands of miles in every direction. The city serves as a hub for eco-tourism and adventure travel, with countless opportunities for visitors to explore the jungle, encounter exotic wildlife, and immerse themselves in indigenous cultures.

One of the most popular attractions near Manaus is the Meeting of the Waters, where the black waters of the Rio Negro and the sandy-colored waters of the Solimões river converge but do not mix for several miles, creating a stunning natural phenomenon that is visible from boats and observation points along the river.

In addition to its natural beauty, Manaus is also home to a thriving cultural scene, with museums, galleries, and cultural centers showcasing the rich history and heritage of the Amazon region. The Museu do Índio, for example, offers insights into the cultures and traditions of the indigenous peoples of the Amazon, while the Museu Casa Eduardo Ribeiro provides a glimpse into the life and times of Manaus during the rubber boom era.

Today, Manaus continues to play a vital role in the Amazon region, serving as a major port and industrial center for the export of timber, minerals, and other natural resources. The city's strategic location and infrastructure also make it an important hub for trade and commerce, connecting the Amazon to markets both domestically and internationally.

But perhaps most importantly, Manaus serves as a reminder of the incredible diversity and ecological importance of the Amazon rainforest, a fragile ecosystem that is home to millions of species of plants and animals, many of which are found nowhere else on Earth. As the gateway to this vast wilderness, Manaus offers visitors a glimpse into a world of unparalleled beauty, wonder, and adventure, inviting them to explore and experience the magic of the Amazon for themselves.

Belém: Historical Port City and Culinary Delights

Belém, situated at the mouth of the Amazon River in the northern state of Pará, is a historical port city known for its rich heritage, vibrant culture, and culinary delights. Founded by the Portuguese in the early 17th century, Belém quickly became one of the most important ports in the region, serving as a gateway to the Amazon and a hub for trade and commerce between Europe, Africa, and the Americas.

One of the most iconic landmarks in Belém is the Ver-o-Peso Market, a bustling marketplace that has been in operation for over 350 years. Here, visitors can browse stalls selling fresh fruits, vegetables, fish, and other local products, as well as handicrafts, souvenirs, and traditional medicines. The market is also home to the Mercado do Peixe, where visitors can sample fresh seafood dishes prepared by local vendors.

Another must-visit attraction in Belém is the historic district of Cidade Velha, or Old Town, which is home to a wealth of colonial-era architecture, including churches, mansions, and government buildings. The São José Fort, built in the 17th century to defend the city from foreign invaders, offers panoramic views of the city and the nearby Guajará Bay.

Belém is also famous for its rich culinary tradition, which blends indigenous, African, and Portuguese influences to create a unique and flavorful cuisine. One of the city's most beloved dishes is tacacá, a savory soup made with jambu leaves, tucupi broth, and dried shrimp, often served in small cups by street vendors throughout the city. Other local delicacies include pato no tucupi (duck in tucupi sauce), maniçoba (a stew made with cassava leaves), and açaí na tigela (açaí served in a bowl with granola and fruit).

In addition to its culinary delights, Belém is also known for its vibrant cultural scene, with museums, theaters, and galleries showcasing the city's rich history and artistic heritage. The Museu Paraense Emílio Goeldi, for example, is a natural history museum and botanical garden that houses over 2.5 million specimens of plants, animals, and fossils from the Amazon region. The Theatro da Paz, built in the late 19th century, is one of the oldest and most beautiful theaters in Brazil, hosting concerts, operas, and theatrical performances throughout the year.

But perhaps the most enduring legacy of Belém is its warm and welcoming spirit, with residents known for their hospitality, friendliness, and joie de vivre. Whether exploring the city's historic landmarks, sampling its culinary delights, or immersing yourself in its vibrant culture, Belém offers a truly unforgettable experience that will leave you enchanted and inspired.

Fortaleza: Sun, Sand, and Surf along the Northeast Coast

Fortaleza, nestled along the stunning northeastern coast of Brazil, is a vibrant city known for its sun-drenched beaches, crystalline waters, and laid-back atmosphere. As the capital of the state of Ceará, Fortaleza attracts visitors from around the world with its irresistible blend of natural beauty, cultural richness, and warm hospitality.

The city's coastline stretches for miles, offering an array of pristine beaches that cater to every taste and preference. Praia do Futuro, one of the most popular beaches in Fortaleza, boasts golden sands, gentle waves, and a lively atmosphere, with beach bars and restaurants serving up fresh seafood and refreshing caipirinhas. Other notable beaches include Praia de Iracema, with its bustling boardwalk and vibrant nightlife, and Praia do Meireles, known for its calm waters and stunning sunset views.

But Fortaleza is more than just a beach destination—it's also a city steeped in history and culture, with a rich heritage that reflects its diverse influences. Founded by the Portuguese in the early 18th century, Fortaleza has a storied past that is evident in its colonial-era architecture, historic landmarks, and vibrant arts scene. The Centro Dragão do Mar de Arte e Cultura, for example, is a cultural center housed in a former prison that showcases contemporary art, music, and theater from Brazil and beyond.

One of the most iconic symbols of Fortaleza is the Ponte dos Ingleses, or English Bridge, a historic structure that spans the mouth of the Pajeú River and offers panoramic views of the coastline. Built in the early 20th century by British engineers, the bridge is a popular spot for strolling, sightseeing, and enjoying the ocean breeze.

Fortaleza is also known for its lively street markets, where visitors can shop for handicrafts, souvenirs, and local delicacies. The Mercado Central, located in the heart of the city, is a bustling market that sells everything from fresh produce and seafood to leather goods and traditional lacework. The Feirinha da Beira-Mar, held along the waterfront promenade, is another popular market where visitors can browse stalls selling handmade crafts, clothing, and jewelry.

But perhaps the biggest draw of Fortaleza is its laid-back vibe and welcoming atmosphere, with residents known for their friendliness, hospitality, and love of life. Whether relaxing on the beach, exploring the city's historic landmarks, or sampling its culinary delights, visitors to Fortaleza are sure to be captivated by its natural beauty, cultural richness, and infectious energy.

Porto Alegre: Gastronomy and Gaúcho Culture in the South

Porto Alegre, situated in the southernmost state of Rio Grande do Sul, is a city celebrated for its rich gastronomy and vibrant Gaúcho culture. As the capital and largest city of Rio Grande do Sul, Porto Alegre is a melting pot of culinary traditions, with influences from Portuguese, indigenous, and immigrant cultures shaping its diverse food scene.

One of the defining features of Porto Alegre's gastronomy is its emphasis on grilled meats, a reflection of the region's strong ranching and cattle-raising heritage. Churrasco, or Brazilian barbecue, is a beloved local tradition, with restaurants and churrascarias serving up succulent cuts of beef, pork, and poultry cooked over open flames on skewers. The Rodízio-style dining experience, where servers circulate among tables offering an endless parade of grilled meats, is a popular way to enjoy churrasco in Porto Alegre.

In addition to churrasco, Porto Alegre is also known for its hearty and flavorful dishes inspired by Gaúcho cuisine. Feijoada, a hearty stew made with black beans and various cuts of pork, is a staple of Brazilian cuisine and a favorite comfort food in Porto Alegre. Other traditional dishes include arroz carreteiro, a rustic rice dish cooked with beef, onions, and spices, and matambre recheado, a rolled beef flank steak stuffed with vegetables and seasonings.

Porto Alegre's culinary scene is also influenced by the city's diverse immigrant populations, with Italian, German, and African influences adding depth and variety to the local food culture. Italian immigrants, for example, brought with them a love of pasta and pizza, while German settlers introduced hearty dishes such as schnitzel and sauerkraut. African influences are evident in dishes like carreteiro de charque, a rice dish made with dried beef, and vatapá, a spicy seafood stew.

But Porto Alegre's gastronomy is not just about hearty meals—it's also about indulging in sweet treats and savory snacks. The city's bakeries and cafes offer a tempting array of pastries, cakes, and desserts, including the iconic chimarrão, a traditional herbal tea served in a gourd and sipped through a metal straw.

Beyond its culinary delights, Porto Alegre is also known for its vibrant Gaúcho culture, which celebrates the traditions, music, and folklore of Rio Grande do Sul. The city hosts numerous festivals and events throughout the year, including the Semana Farroupilha, a week-long celebration of Gaúcho culture that commemorates the state's role in the Farroupilha Revolution.

Whether indulging in savory churrasco, sampling traditional Gaúcho dishes, or immersing oneself in the rich cultural heritage of Rio Grande do Sul, Porto Alegre offers a culinary and cultural experience that is sure to leave a lasting impression on visitors.

Florianópolis: Island Paradise and Surfing Haven

Florianópolis, often referred to as Floripa, is a captivating city located on the southern coast of Brazil, known for its breathtaking natural beauty, vibrant culture, and world-class surfing spots. Situated on the island of Santa Catarina, Florianópolis offers visitors a perfect blend of pristine beaches, lush forests, and charming colonial architecture.

One of the main attractions of Florianópolis is its stunning coastline, which boasts over 40 beaches spread across the island. From popular tourist spots like Praia Mole and Joaquina, known for their excellent surfing conditions and vibrant beach culture, to secluded gems like Lagoinha do Leste and Naufragados, where visitors can enjoy tranquility and untouched nature, there's a beach for every taste and preference in Florianópolis.

In addition to its world-class surfing, Florianópolis is also a paradise for water sports enthusiasts, offering opportunities for snorkeling, diving, windsurfing, and stand-up paddleboarding. The crystal-clear waters and diverse marine life make it an ideal destination for exploring the underwater world and experiencing the thrill of aquatic adventures.

Beyond its beaches, Florianópolis is also known for its rich cultural heritage and lively atmosphere. The city's historic center, located on the mainland, is home to charming cobblestone streets, colorful colonial buildings, and bustling markets, where visitors can immerse themselves in the local culture and sample traditional foods and crafts.

Florianópolis is also a melting pot of cultures, with influences from indigenous peoples, Portuguese settlers, and immigrant communities shaping its unique identity. This diversity is reflected in the city's cuisine, which features a delicious blend of flavors and ingredients from around the world. From fresh seafood and traditional Brazilian dishes to international cuisines and gourmet fare, there's no shortage of culinary delights to discover in Florianópolis.

In addition to its natural beauty and cultural attractions, Florianópolis also offers a vibrant nightlife scene, with beach bars, nightclubs, and live music venues scattered throughout the city. Whether you're looking to dance the night away, enjoy a sunset cocktail by the beach, or simply soak up the local ambiance, Florianópolis has something for everyone.

Overall, Florianópolis is a true island paradise, offering visitors an unparalleled blend of sun, surf, and culture. Whether you're seeking adventure, relaxation, or cultural immersion, Floripa has it all, making it a must-visit destination for travelers from around the world.

Belo Horizonte: Cultural Capital of Minas Gerais

Belo Horizonte, the capital city of the state of Minas Gerais, is a vibrant cultural hub known for its rich history, diverse arts scene, and culinary delights. Situated in the southeastern region of Brazil, Belo Horizonte is the sixth-largest city in the country and a melting pot of cultural influences that reflect its unique heritage.

Founded in the late 19th century as a planned city, Belo Horizonte was designed by urban planners to be a modern metropolis with wide avenues, spacious parks, and grand boulevards. Today, the city's well-planned layout and architectural landmarks, such as the Pampulha Modern Ensemble designed by renowned architect Oscar Niemeyer, are a testament to its forward-thinking urban design.

But beyond its urban landscape, Belo Horizonte is also known for its rich cultural heritage, with a thriving arts scene that encompasses music, theater, dance, and visual arts. The city is home to numerous cultural institutions, including the Palácio das Artes, a cultural complex that hosts concerts, exhibitions, and performances by local and international artists. The Centro Cultural Banco do Brasil, housed in a historic building in the city center, showcases rotating exhibitions of contemporary art and cultural events.

Music is an integral part of life in Belo Horizonte, with the city's vibrant music scene encompassing a wide range of genres, from traditional Brazilian music like samba and choro to rock, jazz, and electronic music. The city's bars, clubs, and concert venues regularly host live music performances by local bands and musicians, making it a mecca for music lovers.

Belo Horizonte is also known for its culinary scene, which celebrates the rich flavors and ingredients of Minas Gerais cuisine. Traditional dishes like feijão tropeiro, tutu de feijão, and pão de queijo are staples of the local diet, while street food vendors serve up delicious snacks like pastéis and coxinhas. The Mercado Central, a bustling marketplace in the heart of the city, is a food lover's paradise, with vendors selling everything from fresh produce and spices to artisanal cheeses and cured meats.

But perhaps the most iconic aspect of Belo Horizonte's cultural identity is its people, known as "mineiros," who are renowned for their warmth, hospitality, and love of life. Whether exploring the city's cultural landmarks, sampling its culinary delights, or simply soaking up the local ambiance, visitors to Belo Horizonte are sure to be enchanted by its rich cultural tapestry and welcoming spirit.

Historical Architecture: Baroque Splendor to Modern Marvels

The historical architecture of Brazil is a tapestry woven with influences from various periods, ranging from baroque splendor to modern marvels. One of the most prominent architectural styles in Brazil is Baroque, which flourished during the colonial period under Portuguese rule. This era left behind a legacy of ornate churches, cathedrals, and palaces adorned with intricate carvings, gilded altars, and colorful tiles known as azulejos.

In cities like Ouro Preto, Salvador, and Recife, visitors can marvel at the grandeur of Baroque architecture, with its elaborate facades and detailed interiors. Ouro Preto, a UNESCO World Heritage Site, is home to some of Brazil's finest examples of Baroque architecture, including the São Francisco de Assis Church and the Church of Saint Francis of Assisi, both adorned with magnificent gold leaf decorations and intricate woodwork.

As Brazil transitioned into the 19th and 20th centuries, architectural styles evolved, reflecting the changing tastes and influences of the time. In Rio de Janeiro, for example, the Belle Époque period saw the construction of iconic landmarks such as the Municipal Theater and the Candelária Church, blending neoclassical, art deco, and eclectic architectural elements.

The early 20th century brought a wave of modernist architecture to Brazil, with pioneering architects like Oscar Niemeyer leading the way. Niemeyer's avant-garde designs, characterized by sweeping curves, bold geometric forms, and the innovative use of reinforced concrete, helped define Brazil's architectural identity and left an indelible mark on cities like Brasília, São Paulo, and Belo Horizonte.

Brasília, the capital city designed by Niemeyer and urban planner Lúcio Costa in the late 1950s, is a masterpiece of modernist architecture, with its sleek government buildings, futuristic monuments, and expansive urban spaces. The city's iconic landmarks, including the National Congress, the Cathedral of Brasília, and the Palácio da Alvorada, showcase Niemeyer's visionary approach to architecture and urban planning.

In recent years, Brazil's architectural landscape has continued to evolve, with contemporary architects blending tradition with innovation to create buildings that are both functional and aesthetically striking. From the striking Museum of Tomorrow in Rio de Janeiro to the sleek São Paulo Museum of Art, Brazil's architectural heritage is a testament to the country's rich cultural heritage and creative spirit.

Indigenous Peoples: Heritage, Identity, and Challenges

The indigenous peoples of Brazil are an integral part of the country's cultural heritage, with a history that spans thousands of years. Before the arrival of European colonizers in the 16th century, Brazil was home to a diverse array of indigenous groups, each with its own languages, traditions, and ways of life. These indigenous peoples inhabited every corner of the country, from the dense Amazon rainforest to the vast plains of the Cerrado and the coastal regions of the Atlantic Forest.

Today, Brazil is home to an estimated 305 distinct indigenous ethnic groups, speaking over 270 different languages. These groups vary widely in size, ranging from small, isolated tribes with just a few dozen members to larger communities with thousands of individuals. Despite their diversity, all indigenous peoples share a deep connection to their ancestral lands and a strong sense of cultural identity.

For centuries, indigenous peoples have faced numerous challenges, including land loss, environmental degradation, and social marginalization. The arrival of European colonizers brought devastating consequences for indigenous communities, including violence, disease, and forced displacement. Many indigenous groups were decimated by diseases like smallpox, measles, and influenza, to which they had no immunity.

Throughout Brazil's history, indigenous peoples have fought to defend their lands and preserve their cultures in the face of ongoing threats. The Brazilian government has recognized indigenous rights to land and resources through the demarcation of indigenous territories, which are protected areas where indigenous communities can live according to their traditional ways of life. However, these territories continue to face encroachment by illegal loggers, miners, and ranchers, leading to conflicts and environmental destruction.

In recent years, indigenous peoples have become increasingly vocal in their demands for land rights, environmental protection, and respect for their cultural heritage. Indigenous leaders and activists have organized protests, legal challenges, and advocacy campaigns to raise awareness of their struggles and push for change. Despite these efforts, indigenous communities continue to face discrimination, poverty, and social exclusion, with many living in remote areas with limited access to basic services like healthcare and education.

Despite the challenges they face, indigenous peoples remain resilient and proud of their heritage. They continue to pass down their traditions, languages, and knowledge to future generations, ensuring that their rich cultural legacy will endure for years to come. As Brazil moves forward, it is essential to recognize and respect the rights of indigenous peoples and work together to build a more inclusive and equitable society for all.

Afro-Brazilian Culture: Contributions and Resilience

Afro-Brazilian culture is a vibrant tapestry woven with the rich traditions, contributions, and resilience of people of African descent in Brazil. The roots of Afro-Brazilian culture can be traced back to the transatlantic slave trade, which brought millions of Africans to Brazil between the 16th and 19th centuries. These enslaved Africans brought with them their languages, religions, music, dance, and culinary traditions, which have profoundly influenced Brazilian culture and society.

One of the most significant contributions of Afro-Brazilian culture is in the realm of music and dance. African rhythms and melodies permeate Brazilian music, from the samba and bossa nova of Rio de Janeiro to the maracatu and frevo of the Northeast. The vibrant beats of the atabaque drums, the twirls of capoeira, a martial art disguised as a dance, and the rhythmic sway of the berimbau are all integral parts of Afro-Brazilian cultural expressions.

Religion also plays a central role in Afro-Brazilian culture, with practices like Candomblé, Umbanda, and Quilombo spirituality blending African, indigenous, and Catholic beliefs. These syncretic religions honor ancestral spirits, deities, and nature, and provide a sense of identity and community for Afro-Brazilian communities across the country. Rituals, ceremonies, and festivals, such as the Festival of Iemanjá, celebrate the African heritage and promote cultural continuity and resilience.

Afro-Brazilian culture has also made significant contributions to Brazilian cuisine, with dishes like feijoada, acarajé, moqueca, and vatapá originating from African culinary traditions. These dishes, which combine ingredients like beans, rice, seafood, and spices, reflect the diversity and richness of Afro-Brazilian gastronomy and are enjoyed by people of all backgrounds throughout Brazil.

Despite centuries of oppression, discrimination, and marginalization, Afro-Brazilian culture remains vibrant and resilient, with Afro-Brazilians making important contributions to all aspects of Brazilian society. From politics and literature to art and sports, Afro-Brazilians have played a vital role in shaping the identity and cultural landscape of Brazil.

However, challenges persist, including systemic racism, economic inequality, and social injustice, which continue to disproportionately affect Afro-Brazilian communities. Movements for racial equality and social justice, such as the Black Consciousness Movement and the Quilombola Movement, continue to advocate for the rights and empowerment of Afro-Brazilians and work to dismantle structures of oppression and discrimination.

As Brazil continues to grapple with its complex history and strive towards a more inclusive and equitable society, the resilience, creativity, and contributions of Afro-Brazilian culture serve as a powerful reminder of the strength and resilience of the human spirit. Afro-Brazilian culture is not just a part of Brazil's past; it is a living, breathing expression of identity, heritage, and pride that continues to inspire and enrich the nation.

Urbanization and Megacities: Challenges and Opportunities

Urbanization and the rise of megacities present both challenges and opportunities for Brazil and its people. As the country's population continues to grow, more and more people are flocking to cities in search of better opportunities, leading to rapid urbanization and the proliferation of megacities.

São Paulo, Rio de Janeiro, and Brasília are among Brazil's largest and most populous cities, each facing unique challenges and opportunities as they grapple with the complexities of urban life. São Paulo, for example, is a bustling metropolis known for its vibrant culture, economic dynamism, and diversity. However, it also faces serious issues such as traffic congestion, air pollution, and socioeconomic inequality.

Rio de Janeiro, with its stunning natural beauty and world-famous landmarks like the Christ the Redeemer statue and Copacabana Beach, is a major tourist destination and cultural center. However, it also struggles with high crime rates, inadequate public services, and social disparities between affluent and marginalized neighborhoods.

Brasília, the capital city designed by Oscar Niemeyer in the 1950s, is a symbol of modernist architecture and urban planning. Its spacious boulevards, futuristic buildings, and expansive green spaces reflect Brazil's aspirations for progress and development. However, like other Brazilian cities, Brasília also faces challenges such as urban sprawl, informal settlements, and environmental degradation.

One of the biggest challenges of urbanization is providing adequate housing, infrastructure, and services for growing urban populations. In many Brazilian cities, informal settlements known as favelas have sprung up to accommodate migrants from rural areas and other parts of the country. These settlements often lack basic amenities like running water, sanitation, and electricity, leading to poor living conditions and health disparities.

Another challenge is ensuring sustainable urban development that balances economic growth with environmental conservation and social equity. Rapid urbanization can strain natural resources, increase pollution, and exacerbate climate change, posing risks to both urban and rural communities. However, cities also offer opportunities for innovation, entrepreneurship, and cultural exchange, driving economic growth and social progress.

Efforts to address these challenges include urban planning initiatives, affordable housing programs, and investments in public transportation, education, and healthcare. Sustainable development goals, such as the United Nations' Agenda 2030, provide a framework for cities to promote inclusive, resilient, and sustainable urbanization.

Ultimately, the future of Brazil's cities depends on their ability to harness the opportunities of urbanization while addressing the challenges it brings. By investing in infrastructure, promoting social inclusion, and protecting the environment, Brazilian cities can become engines of growth, innovation, and prosperity for generations to come.

Conservation Efforts: Preserving Brazil's Natural Heritage

Conservation efforts in Brazil are crucial for preserving the country's vast and diverse natural heritage, which includes the Amazon rainforest, the Pantanal wetlands, the Atlantic Forest, and numerous other ecosystems teeming with biodiversity. Brazil is home to approximately 20% of the world's known species, making it one of the most biodiverse countries on the planet.

The Amazon rainforest, often referred to as the "lungs of the Earth," plays a vital role in regulating the global climate and storing carbon dioxide. However, deforestation and forest degradation pose significant threats to the Amazon, driven by activities such as agriculture, logging, mining, and infrastructure development. In response, Brazil has implemented various conservation initiatives, including protected areas, indigenous territories, and sustainable development projects aimed at reducing deforestation and promoting sustainable land use practices.

The establishment of protected areas, such as national parks, biological reserves, and extractive reserves, has been instrumental in safeguarding Brazil's biodiversity and ecosystems. These protected areas cover over 17% of Brazil's territory and provide habitat for thousands of plant and animal species, including endangered species like the jaguar, the giant anteater, and the harpy eagle.

Indigenous peoples also play a crucial role in conservation efforts in Brazil, as many indigenous territories overlap with areas of high biodiversity and ecological significance. Indigenous communities have a deep connection to their ancestral lands and often serve as stewards of the environment, practicing traditional sustainable land management techniques that help preserve biodiversity and protect natural resources.

Brazil has also made significant strides in combating illegal deforestation and environmental crime through law enforcement efforts, satellite monitoring, and partnerships with international organizations and governments. The Brazilian government has implemented policies such as the Soy Moratorium and the Cattle Agreement, which aim to reduce deforestation associated with soybean cultivation and cattle ranching, two leading drivers of deforestation in the Amazon.

Despite these efforts, conservation challenges persist in Brazil, including illegal logging, land grabbing, wildfires, and the expansion of agribusiness into sensitive ecosystems. Climate change also poses a growing threat to Brazil's biodiversity, with rising temperatures, changing rainfall patterns, and extreme weather events affecting ecosystems and wildlife.

To address these challenges, conservationists, scientists, policymakers, and local communities must work together to develop innovative solutions that balance conservation with sustainable development and address the underlying drivers of deforestation and environmental degradation. By investing in conservation, Brazil can protect its natural heritage for future generations and contribute to global efforts to preserve biodiversity and combat climate change.

Economic Powerhouses: Industries Driving Brazil's Growth

In Brazil, several key industries drive the nation's economic growth and contribute significantly to its status as one of the world's largest economies. One of the most prominent sectors is agriculture, which accounts for a significant portion of Brazil's GDP and exports. Brazil is a major producer and exporter of commodities such as soybeans, sugarcane, coffee, beef, and poultry, thanks to its vast arable land, favorable climate, and advanced agricultural technology. The agricultural sector not only generates revenue but also provides employment opportunities for millions of Brazilians, particularly in rural areas.

Another major industry in Brazil is the automotive sector, which has experienced significant growth and development over the years. Brazil is one of the world's largest producers and consumers of automobiles, with major manufacturers like Volkswagen, General Motors, and Fiat Chrysler Automobiles operating production facilities in the country. The automotive industry contributes to Brazil's industrial output, exports, and job creation, supporting a vast network of suppliers, dealerships, and service providers across the country.

The mining industry is also a significant contributor to Brazil's economy, particularly in terms of exports and foreign exchange earnings. Brazil is rich in mineral resources, including iron ore, bauxite, gold, copper, and nickel, which are extracted and processed by multinational mining companies such as Vale, Anglo American, and BHP. The mining sector generates revenue, investment, and employment opportunities, particularly in regions like Minas Gerais, Pará, and Goiás, where mineral deposits are abundant.

The energy sector is another key driver of Brazil's economy, with the country being a global leader in renewable energy production, particularly hydropower. Brazil's extensive network of rivers and abundant rainfall make it well-suited for hydroelectric power generation, with large-scale projects like the Itaipu Dam and the Belo Monte Dam contributing significantly to the country's electricity supply. In addition to hydropower, Brazil also invests in other renewable energy sources such as wind, solar, and biomass, as part of its efforts to diversify its energy mix and reduce carbon emissions.

The services sector is the largest contributor to Brazil's GDP, encompassing a wide range of industries such as finance, telecommunications, retail, tourism, and entertainment. Cities like São Paulo and Rio de Janeiro serve as major financial and commercial centers, hosting headquarters of multinational corporations, banks, and investment firms. The services sector provides employment opportunities for millions of Brazilians and contributes to the country's economic growth and development.

Overall, these industries, along with others like manufacturing, technology, and healthcare, play vital roles in driving Brazil's economic growth, creating jobs, and fostering innovation and development. However, challenges such as infrastructure deficiencies, bureaucratic hurdles, and economic inequality persist, requiring concerted efforts from government, businesses, and civil society to address and overcome.

Social Inequality: Addressing Challenges of Poverty and Inequity

Social inequality is a pressing issue in Brazil, marked by significant disparities in income, education, healthcare, and access to basic services. Despite being one of the world's largest economies, Brazil struggles with high levels of poverty and inequity, which disproportionately affect marginalized communities, including Afro-Brazilians, indigenous peoples, women, and residents of rural areas and urban slums.

Income inequality in Brazil is among the highest in the world, with a small elite controlling a disproportionate share of the country's wealth and resources. According to the World Bank, the wealthiest 1% of the population in Brazil holds around 28% of the country's total income, while the poorest 50% holds less than 10%. This stark wealth gap reflects historical legacies of slavery, colonialism, and structural discrimination that continue to shape Brazil's social and economic landscape.

Poverty remains a pervasive problem in Brazil, despite significant progress in reducing poverty rates over the past two decades. According to the Brazilian Institute of Geography and Statistics (IBGE), approximately 21% of the population lived below the national poverty line in 2019, with higher rates in the Northeast and North regions of the country. Rural areas and urban slums, known as favelas, are particularly affected by poverty, lacking access to adequate housing, sanitation, healthcare, and education.

Education is a key determinant of social mobility and opportunity in Brazil, but disparities in educational access and quality persist. Many children from low-income families face barriers to accessing quality education due to factors such as inadequate school infrastructure, teacher shortages, and lack of resources. According to UNESCO, around 2.8 million children and adolescents in Brazil were out of school in 2019, with higher rates among Afro-Brazilians, indigenous peoples, and residents of rural areas.

Healthcare is another area where social inequality is pronounced in Brazil. While the country has a publicly funded universal healthcare system, known as the Unified Health System (SUS), access to healthcare services varies widely depending on factors such as income, location, and ethnicity. Wealthier Brazilians often rely on private healthcare providers, which offer higher-quality services and shorter wait times, while poorer Brazilians depend on the public system, which can be overburdened and under-resourced.

Addressing social inequality in Brazil requires a comprehensive and multi-faceted approach that addresses the root causes of poverty and inequity. This includes investing in education, healthcare, infrastructure, and social programs to ensure that all Brazilians have equal opportunities to thrive and succeed. It also requires tackling systemic discrimination, promoting social inclusion, and empowering marginalized communities to participate fully in the country's social, economic, and political life.

Efforts to reduce social inequality in Brazil have been made through government initiatives such as the Bolsa Família cash transfer program, which provides financial assistance to low-income families, and affirmative action policies that aim to increase access to education and employment for historically marginalized groups. However, more needs to be done to tackle the deep-rooted structural inequalities that continue to perpetuate poverty and inequity in Brazilian society. By addressing these challenges head-on, Brazil can build a more just, inclusive, and prosperous future for all its citizens.

Education and Innovation: Nurturing Talent and Potential

Education and innovation are foundational pillars of Brazil's development, shaping the country's future and driving progress in various sectors. Brazil recognizes the importance of nurturing talent and potential through robust educational systems that foster creativity, critical thinking, and entrepreneurship.

The Brazilian education system comprises public and private institutions at all levels, including preschool, primary school, secondary school, and higher education. Despite significant strides in increasing access to education in recent decades, challenges remain in ensuring quality and equity across the board. Rural areas, urban slums, and marginalized communities often face barriers to accessing quality education due to factors such as inadequate infrastructure, teacher shortages, and socio-economic disparities.

Primary and secondary education in Brazil is compulsory and free for all children aged 6 to 14, with the government investing heavily in expanding school infrastructure, providing textbooks, and training teachers. However, educational outcomes vary widely depending on factors such as location, income level, and ethnicity. Rural schools and schools in low-income areas tend to have lower academic performance and higher dropout rates compared to urban schools and schools in wealthier neighborhoods.

Higher education in Brazil has also expanded significantly in recent decades, with a growing number of universities, colleges, and technical institutes offering a wide range of programs and courses. The Brazilian government has implemented affirmative action policies, such as quotas for students from low-income families, indigenous communities, and Afro-Brazilian descent, to promote access and diversity in higher education.

Brazil is also investing in research and innovation to drive economic growth and competitiveness in the global market. The country has a strong network of research institutions, including universities, research centers, and technology parks, which conduct cutting-edge research in fields such as agriculture, biotechnology, renewable energy, and information technology.

One of Brazil's flagship innovation initiatives is the Brazilian Agency for Industrial Research and Innovation (EMBRAPII), which funds collaborative research projects between academia and industry to develop innovative technologies and products. EMBRAPII focuses on priority areas such as advanced manufacturing, health sciences, and digital transformation, leveraging Brazil's scientific expertise and industrial capabilities to drive innovation and economic development.

In addition to government initiatives, Brazil's private sector plays a crucial role in fostering innovation through investments in research and development, technology startups, and entrepreneurship. Cities like São Paulo, Rio de Janeiro, and Belo Horizonte are emerging as hubs for innovation and technology, attracting talent, capital, and partnerships from around the world.

Overall, education and innovation are essential drivers of Brazil's social and economic development, helping to unlock the country's vast potential and create opportunities for its people. By investing in education, promoting research and innovation, and fostering a culture of creativity and entrepreneurship, Brazil can continue to thrive and compete in the global knowledge economy.

Healthcare System: Access, Challenges, and Advances

The healthcare system in Brazil is a complex network of public and private providers, aiming to ensure access to healthcare services for all citizens. Brazil's healthcare system is governed by the Unified Health System (SUS), a publicly funded and universal healthcare system that guarantees access to healthcare services free of charge at the point of delivery. The SUS was established in 1988 with the promulgation of Brazil's Constitution and is based on the principles of universality, equity, and comprehensiveness.

Under the SUS, healthcare services are provided through a decentralized network of health facilities, including primary care clinics, hospitals, emergency rooms, and specialized treatment centers. The SUS is responsible for providing a wide range of services, including preventive care, medical consultations, diagnostic tests, surgeries, and emergency care. Additionally, the SUS supports public health initiatives, such as vaccination campaigns, disease surveillance, and health promotion programs aimed at preventing illness and promoting well-being.

Despite the achievements of the SUS in expanding access to healthcare services, Brazil's healthcare system faces significant challenges, including underfunding, unequal distribution of resources, and disparities in access to care. While the SUS aims to provide universal healthcare coverage, access to quality healthcare services varies across regions and population groups. Rural areas, indigenous communities, and urban slums often face barriers to accessing healthcare due to factors such as geographical isolation, limited infrastructure, and socioeconomic inequalities.

Brazil's healthcare system also struggles with capacity constraints, particularly in terms of hospital beds, medical equipment, and healthcare professionals. The country faces shortages of doctors, nurses, and other healthcare workers, particularly in remote areas and underserved regions. Additionally, the SUS often experiences long wait times for medical appointments and surgeries, leading some patients to seek care in the private healthcare sector, where services are often faster but come with out-of-pocket costs.

To address these challenges, Brazil has implemented various healthcare reforms and initiatives aimed at strengthening the SUS and improving healthcare delivery. These include investments in infrastructure, equipment, and human resources; expansion of primary care services and community health programs; and efforts to improve healthcare management and coordination at the local, regional, and national levels.

In recent years, Brazil has also made significant advances in healthcare technology and innovation, with the development of telemedicine, electronic health records, and digital health platforms aimed at improving access to healthcare services and enhancing patient care. Additionally, Brazil has emerged as a leader in medical research and development, particularly in areas such as tropical medicine, infectious diseases, and public health.

Overall, while Brazil's healthcare system faces challenges, it also presents opportunities for improvement and innovation. By addressing issues of funding, infrastructure, and access, Brazil can work towards achieving the goal of providing high-quality, affordable healthcare for all its citizens.

Tourism Highlights: Must-See Destinations and Attractions

Brazil is a land of diverse landscapes, vibrant culture, and rich history, making it a top destination for travelers from around the world. From the bustling streets of Rio de Janeiro to the pristine beaches of Fernando de Noronha, Brazil offers a wide range of attractions and experiences for every type of traveler.

One of Brazil's most iconic tourist destinations is Rio de Janeiro, famous for its stunning beaches, lively Carnival celebrations, and iconic landmarks such as Christ the Redeemer and Sugarloaf Mountain. Visitors can soak up the sun on the golden sands of Copacabana and Ipanema beaches, explore the historic neighborhood of Santa Teresa, or take a cable car ride to the top of Sugarloaf Mountain for panoramic views of the city.

Another must-see destination in Brazil is the Amazon Rainforest, one of the most biodiverse regions on Earth. Travelers can embark on guided tours and river cruises to explore the lush jungle, spot exotic wildlife such as jaguars and monkeys, and learn about the indigenous cultures that call the Amazon home. The city of Manaus serves as the gateway to the Amazon, offering access to the surrounding rainforest as well as cultural attractions such as the Amazon Theatre and the Meeting of Waters.

For those seeking adventure and natural beauty, Brazil's Pantanal region is a must-visit destination. The Pantanal is the world's largest tropical wetland, home to a staggering array of wildlife, including caimans, capybaras, and giant otters. Visitors can embark on guided safaris, boat tours, and horseback riding excursions to explore the vast marshlands and encounter the region's diverse fauna and flora.

In addition to its natural wonders, Brazil is also home to a wealth of cultural attractions and historic sites. The historic city of Salvador, located in the northeastern state of Bahia, is known for its Afro-Brazilian culture, colorful colonial architecture, and lively music and dance scene. Visitors can explore the historic Pelourinho district, visit the São Francisco Church and Convent of Salvador, or attend a traditional capoeira performance.

Other must-see destinations in Brazil include the colonial town of Ouro Preto, known for its well-preserved baroque architecture and historic churches; the spectacular Iguazu Falls, which straddle the border between Brazil and Argentina; and the remote paradise islands of Fernando de Noronha, renowned for their pristine beaches and crystal-clear waters teeming with marine life.

Whether you're drawn to Brazil's natural beauty, rich cultural heritage, or vibrant cities, the country offers an unforgettable travel experience that is sure to leave a lasting impression. From the towering waterfalls of Iguaçu to the rhythms of samba in Rio, Brazil is a destination that truly has something for everyone.

Iguazu Falls: Natural Wonder Shared with Argentina

Iguazu Falls, located on the border between Brazil and Argentina, is one of the most awe-inspiring natural wonders in the world. This magnificent waterfall system consists of a series of 275 individual cascades spread across a nearly 2-mile stretch of the Iguazu River, creating a spectacle of unparalleled beauty and power.

The falls are situated within two national parks: Iguazú National Park in Argentina and Iguaçu National Park in Brazil, both of which have been designated UNESCO World Heritage Sites for their outstanding natural value. The surrounding rainforest ecosystems are home to an incredible diversity of plant and animal species, including jaguars, toucans, and orchids, making the area a haven for nature lovers and wildlife enthusiasts.

One of the most iconic features of Iguazu Falls is the Devil's Throat (Garganta del Diablo or Garganta do Diabo), a massive U-shaped waterfall that spans nearly 490 feet in width and plunges over 260 feet into the chasm below. Standing on viewing platforms overlooking the Devil's Throat, visitors are treated to a breathtaking panorama of cascading water and swirling mist, creating a sensory experience that is both exhilarating and humbling.

Visitors to Iguazu Falls can explore the falls from both the Brazilian and Argentine sides, each offering unique perspectives and vantage points. On the Brazilian side, visitors can take a scenic walk along elevated walkways that offer panoramic views of the falls and surrounding rainforest, allowing for up-close encounters with the rushing water and vibrant flora and fauna.

On the Argentine side, visitors can embark on a series of walking trails and boardwalks that lead to various viewpoints overlooking the falls, including the iconic Devil's Throat. Boat tours and adventure activities such as rafting and zip-lining are also available for those seeking a more adrenaline-fueled experience.

The region surrounding Iguazu Falls is also rich in cultural heritage, with indigenous Guarani communities inhabiting the area for centuries. Visitors can learn about the indigenous history and culture of the region through guided tours, cultural performances, and visits to local craft markets.

Overall, Iguazu Falls is a testament to the raw power and beauty of nature, offering visitors an unforgettable experience that showcases the best of South America's natural wonders. Whether viewed from the Brazilian side or the Argentine side, Iguazu Falls is a must-see destination for anyone exploring the diverse landscapes and rich biodiversity of the continent.

Christ the Redeemer and Sugarloaf Mountain: Rio's Icons

Christ the Redeemer and Sugarloaf Mountain are two iconic landmarks that define the skyline of Rio de Janeiro, Brazil's vibrant and bustling coastal city. These architectural marvels not only offer breathtaking views of the city and its surroundings but also hold cultural and historical significance for both locals and visitors alike.

Christ the Redeemer, or Cristo Redentor in Portuguese, is a colossal statue of Jesus Christ that stands atop the summit of Corcovado Mountain, overlooking the city of Rio de Janeiro. Standing at a height of 98 feet (30 meters), with its outstretched arms spanning 92 feet (28 meters) wide, the statue is one of the largest and most recognizable religious monuments in the world. It was constructed between 1922 and 1931 as a symbol of Brazilian Christianity and a gesture of peace and unity.

The statue of Christ the Redeemer is made of reinforced concrete and soapstone and was designed by Brazilian engineer Heitor da Silva Costa and French sculptor Paul Landowski. It has become a symbol of Rio de Janeiro and Brazil as a whole, attracting millions of visitors each year who come to admire its imposing presence and panoramic views of the city and surrounding landscape.

Sugarloaf Mountain, known locally as Pão de Açúcar, is another iconic landmark that rises dramatically from the shores of Guanabara Bay, offering stunning views of Rio de Janeiro and its famous beaches. The mountain is named for its resemblance to the traditional shape of a loaf of sugar, with its steep cliffs and rocky outcrops towering over the city below.

Visitors to Sugarloaf Mountain can reach the summit via a series of cable cars that transport them to two separate peaks, providing 360-degree views of Rio de Janeiro, including the sparkling waters of Guanabara Bay, the lush greenery of Tijuca National Park, and the iconic beaches of Copacabana and Ipanema. The cable car ride itself is an exhilarating experience, offering breathtaking views of the cityscape and surrounding landscape as it ascends to the summit.

Both Christ the Redeemer and Sugarloaf Mountain are UNESCO World Heritage Sites and are considered must-visit attractions for anyone traveling to Rio de Janeiro. Whether admiring the sunset from the top of Sugarloaf Mountain or gazing out over the city from the feet of Christ the Redeemer, visitors are sure to be captivated by the beauty and majesty of these iconic landmarks.

The Pantanal: Wetland Wilderness and Wildlife Sanctuary

The Pantanal is a vast tropical wetland region located primarily in Brazil, extending into portions of Bolivia and Paraguay. It is the world's largest tropical wetland area, covering an estimated area of over 70,000 square miles (180,000 square kilometers) during the wet season. The Pantanal is renowned for its incredible biodiversity and is often referred to as one of the most diverse ecosystems on the planet.

This unique region is characterized by its seasonal flooding, with water levels fluctuating dramatically between the wet and dry seasons. During the wet season, from November to March, large portions of the Pantanal become inundated with water, creating a vast network of interconnected rivers, lakes, and marshes. This flooding is essential for the region's ecology, providing vital habitat for a wide variety of aquatic and terrestrial species.

One of the most remarkable aspects of the Pantanal is its incredible diversity of wildlife. The region is home to an estimated 1,000 species of birds, 400 species of fish, 300 species of mammals, and 480 species of reptiles and amphibians. Among the most iconic residents of the Pantanal are the jaguar, the largest cat species in the Americas, which preys on the abundant populations of capybaras, caimans, and marsh deer that inhabit the wetlands.

In addition to jaguars, the Pantanal is also home to a wide variety of other large mammals, including giant otters, tapirs, and anteaters. The region's extensive network of waterways provides habitat for a rich diversity of aquatic species, including piranhas, anacondas, and the critically endangered giant river otter.

The Pantanal is also a paradise for birdwatchers, with hundreds of species of birds found within its borders. From colorful macaws and toucans to majestic raptors and storks, the Pantanal offers unparalleled opportunities for birdwatching enthusiasts to observe and photograph a diverse array of avian species in their natural habitat.

In recent years, the Pantanal has faced significant threats from deforestation, agriculture, and climate change, leading to concerns about the long-term health and sustainability of this unique ecosystem. Conservation efforts are underway to protect and preserve the Pantanal's natural resources and biodiversity, including the establishment of protected areas and sustainable management practices.

Despite these challenges, the Pantanal remains one of the most ecologically important and biologically diverse regions in the world, offering visitors a truly unforgettable wilderness experience unlike any other. Whether exploring its vast wetlands by boat, trekking through its dense forests, or observing its abundant wildlife from a safe distance, the Pantanal continues to captivate and inspire all who venture into its wild and untamed landscapes.

Epilogue

In closing, Brazil stands as a country of immense diversity and vitality, woven with a tapestry of cultures, landscapes, and histories that make it truly unique on the global stage. From the dense Amazon rainforest to the vibrant cities of Rio de Janeiro and São Paulo, Brazil offers a wealth of experiences and opportunities for exploration.

Throughout its history, Brazil has weathered numerous challenges and triumphs, from colonial rule to independence, from political upheavals to economic growth. Its rich cultural heritage, influenced by indigenous, African, European, and Asian traditions, reflects the complex interplay of peoples and cultures that have shaped the nation's identity.

Today, Brazil is a dynamic and multifaceted society, home to a population of over 200 million people who represent a mosaic of ethnicities, religions, and languages. Its economy, driven by agriculture, industry, and services, ranks among the largest in the world, while its natural beauty and biodiversity continue to attract millions of visitors from around the globe.

As Brazil looks to the future, it faces both opportunities and challenges. The country must navigate issues of social inequality, environmental conservation, and economic development while preserving its cultural heritage and fostering innovation and growth. By harnessing its diverse talents and resources, Brazil has the potential to emerge as a global leader in the 21st century, contributing to the advancement of humanity and the protection of our planet.

In this epilogue, we reflect on Brazil's past, present, and future, celebrating its achievements and acknowledging the work that lies ahead. As we bid farewell to this journey through the vibrant tapestry of Brazil, may we carry with us a deeper understanding and appreciation for this remarkable nation and its people. And may we continue to cherish and protect the treasures that make Brazil a beacon of hope and inspiration for generations to come.

Made in the USA
Las Vegas, NV
01 June 2024

90603972R00059